Family Fun and Games

A Hundred Year Tradition

By

Carolyn Gray Thornton

And

Ellen Gray Massey

Illustrated by LaShelle Oursbourn

Skyward Publishing, Inc.
Dallas, Texas
www.skywardpublishing.com
skyward@sheltonbbs.com

Copyright 2002 by Skyward Publishing, Inc.

Publisher: Skyward Publishing, Inc
            Marketing
            813 Michael Street
            Kennett, MO 63857
            Phone 573-717-1040
            Fax: 413-702-5141
    Email: skyward@sheltonbbs.com
    Web Site: www.skywardpublishing.com

    Library of Congress Cataloging-in-Publication Data
Thornton, Carolyn Gray, 1925-
    Family fun and games: a hundred-year tradition / by
Carolyn Gray Thornton and Ellen Gray Massey;
illustrated by LaShelle Oursbourn.
            p. cm.
    Includes bibliographical references (p.) and index.
    ISBN 1-881554-09-0
    1. Family recreation. 2. Games. I Massey, Ellen Gray.
II. Title.
 GV182.7 . T46 2000
 790.1'91--dc21

Family Fun and Games

A Hundred Year Tradition

Ellen Gray Massey

ATTENTION SCHOOLS AND CORPORATIONS

Skyward Publishing books are available at quantity discount with bulk purchase for educational, business, or sales promotional use. For information contact:

Skyward Publishing, Inc.
Marketing
813 Michael Street
Kennett, Missouri 63857
(573) 717-1040
Email: skyward@sheltonbbs.com

*To our parents, Chester and Pearl Gray, and
all coming after them who inherited their
love of family and of games.*

*An early Gray family reunion in 1948 includes front row,
from left, Ellen, Chester (father), Pearl (mother) and
Carolyn. Second row, from left, Ralph, Vernon, Harold,
Kathryn, Gertrude and Miriam.*

CONTENTS

ABOUT THE AUTHORS

Ellen Gray Massey, left, and Carolyn Gray Thornton, at the entrance to the family farm, The Wayside, in Missouri, near Nevada. (Photo by Vicki Cox)

Carolyn Gray Thornton, a retired social worker, mother, grandmother and great-grandmother, has spent years as the wife of a United Methodist Minister leading games, creating mixers for groups and having fun with all ages of people. With her family background of years of game playing, she has created a program which she presents to Elderhostel groups entitled, "The

Heritage of Games in the Family Culture." This book is a natural outgrowth of her family, professional and volunteer activities in recreational activities. An earlier book, *"A Funny Thing Happened on the Road to Senility"* also published by Skyward Publishing, portrays her appreciation for the enjoyment and fun that can be found in each stage of life. She and her now retired husband live next door to the family farm near Nevada, Missouri where her game playing began when she was a toddler.

Ellen Gray Massey has led games for many diverse groups — her large extended family, 4-H Clubs, recreation workshops, women's groups, her school classes from grade one through graduate school, and more recently at Elderhostel classes.

She is the author of eleven novels and two nonfiction books as well as editor of several anthologies. From 1973-1983 she was the teacher/advisor of *Bittersweet, the Ozark Quarterly*, published by her students at Lebanon High School. She has received two Golden Spur Finalist awards from Western Writers of America, and seven first place ratings in biography, fiction, and feature writing from the Missouri Writers Guild.

She presently lives in Lebanon, Missouri, where she continues to write.

Foreword

"The Widow Jones died last night," Ellen says after dinner at a small gathering that includes five-year-old Marilyn.

"How'd she die?" Penny, Marilyn's mother asks, grinning at her great-aunt for thinking of a game that would include her little daughter who is now old enough to participate.

"Going like this," Ellen says, thumping her right foot up and down without stopping. Marilyn giggles and imitates by stomping her foot. The game continues around the circle of relatives with each in turn following Ellen as she adds new actions. The group is soon rolling with laughter.

The Gray family has always enjoyed games. Whenever any members of our family get together, we end up playing, whether it is at one of the big family reunions of seventy or eighty relatives or just Ellen visiting Carolyn's family. This tradition, which began with our parents, has lasted one hundred years.

A few years ago, after an exciting game-playing session including several families gathered at The Wayside, our farm home in Missouri, Mary Dudley asked her aunts, Ellen and Carolyn, "Why don't you two put all these games into a book for other families to use?"

Mary, a child and family development specialist, knew the value of playing games and also how playing had strengthened the bonds of the Gray family. She explained the need for a book of games with a focus on family — simple ones that can be played together by all ages, just as the Gray family has been doing for five generations.

Game-playing leadership passed down in our family from our parents through our brothers and sisters to us, the youngest of eight siblings. Our professions also included leading games with youth and adult groups. Therefore, we were usually the ones who spear-headed the family game-playing.

The games we have included are not original, though we may have adapted some to better suit our family. We have selected games that have worked — those that have been tested in the laboratory of our family, beginning with our parents and their eight children. The family now extends to grandchildren, great-grandchildren and great-great-grandchildren who live from Connecticut to Oregon and from Minnesota to Texas.

Since part of the value of playing the games is the spontaneity, the games included in Sections II and III need no special equipment or elaborate pre-planning. They are games for anyone, anytime, anywhere. While Monopoly, Twister, Scrabble, and other commercial games, as well as computer games and card games, have value, we omitted them because they include the rules with the purchases. The family has enjoyed many afternoons of croquet, volleyball and frisbee, but these sporting activities are well known and not included. We had to draw the line somewhere.

Section IV gives ideas for successful game-playing with larger gatherings of friends. We include entertainment ideas that require originality, planning, and perhaps even elaborate equipment or supplies. Because we do much more than provide food and background music, guests at our parties remember the fun they have. At these gathering, since our friends are temporarily part of our extended family, we all play together.

Section V focuses on big occasions when people come together because of family or other like interests. It includes the planning needed ahead of time and various details of the gathering to make it an enjoyable success.

The focus of On Your Mark, Get Set, Go! is to provide a resource that will encourage other families to have the experiences the Gray family has enjoyed by playing games that include pre-schoolers to those in their nineties. If youngsters do not understand all subtleties, they are still part of the group. Even if the older aunt does not physically participate, she can enjoy watching the others as they cavort around the lawn in active games.

As children in the Gray family, we brothers and sisters with our parents enjoyed being together. None of us disappeared into our rooms. Even if we had wanted to be alone, we couldn't find a room that didn't include one of the siblings! Ralph and Vernon kept us laughing with their antics. Gertrude never went off by herself. "I was afraid I'd miss something," she said. Harold didn't marry until he was thirty. He jokingly said, "I was having too much fun at home." Kathryn, the first to marry and leave home cried on her honeymoon trip because she realized for the first time that she was leaving her family. Miriam came home for every holiday during her years of teaching.

The unity in the Gray family is built through the frequent opportunities we have made to be together, as well as pride in our parents, in each other, and in our farm, The Wayside. But our tradition of playing games is probably the most enriching.

In the 1960s, grinning at Dorothy, his wife, Vernon would say, "I am somebody." Jane, Ann, and Beth were beginning to tire from the tedious hours of traveling from their Ohio home to visit the grandparents at The Wayside.

Jane immediately knew he was starting a game. "Are you a man?"

Without a pause, Ann asked, "Are you famous?"

"Are you living?" Beth asked.

Vernon answered yes for all. Quiet reigned. The girls smiled and hardly noticed the miles as they asked more questions to figure out who their father was thinking of.

Today when traveling, Beth and Merle ask

their sons the same question. The game begins and Brad quits poking Jeff.

We hope that this book about the heritage our parents gave us will help others create the same tradition in their families.

Carolyn Gray Thornton and
Ellen Gray Massey

1

On Your Mark, Get Set, Go!

On Your Mark, Get Set, Go!

"Let's do something!" eight-year-old Carolyn pipes up with her usual request.

Papa smiles because he, too, is always ready for a game. "Pearl," he says to Mama, "get me your thimble." Carolyn jumps up to help. Everyone in the room knows he is starting a favorite game.

On a quiet Sunday afternoon during the 1930s, the Gray family is enjoying a lazy afternoon in the living room of their home in Washington, D.C. with visiting cousin, Lillian and her husband, Jep. The men set aside their sections of *The Washington Post*. Kathryn and Gertrude join them after washing the dishes following their mother's usual dinner of roast beef, potatoes and gravy, and homemade apple pie.

Papa takes the thimble as everyone leaves the room, including the older siblings who are in their twenties, the visiting cousins, and even Mama. Since the rules say the thimble must be hidden in plain sight, Papa takes advantage of his height to insert the thimble in a link of the chain that holds the ceiling light fixture. He takes his seat near the fireplace and calls for everyone to return.

Since no one spies the thimble for a few minutes, he starts giving hints by saying who is "warmest" and who is really "freezing to death" by their distance from the thimble. Six-foot-tall Ralph notices the thimble but to avoid giving away the hiding place, moves to the other side of the room before saying, "I spy." Kathryn asks, "How can you see that little thimble when you never see all the dirty dishes on the table?"

One family member after another locates the thimble. To help Carolyn, Papa gives her a few extra clues.

Sixty-five years later, on an equally quiet Sunday afternoon Carolyn's son, Michael, and daughter, Shirley, and their families relax after her special pot roast dinner. She hides her own thimble to start the game for her great-granddaughters. The children leave the computer games, ignore the television, and put aside toys that talk back to join in this group game with all ages playing together.

Some Historical Facts about Games

Game playing is older than history. Early cave drawings, preserving a glimpse into prehistoric customs, show that primitive peoples played games. Perhaps games are the re-enactment of the childhood of the human race. Their value has been recognized for centuries since games create the opportunity for the child's first group activity.

The singing and acting game of Oats and Beans and Barley Grow has its origins in pre-historic fertility rites during spring planting. The Mulberry Bush, beloved by every kindergartner, is a survival of the ancient spring festival dances in which players encircled a sacred bush. Ring Around the Rosie comes from the plague years in Europe. People believed that rose petals warded off the disease when they burned those who died.

Tag has its origin in adult flight from an evil spirit from whom the person was safe if he touched wood. Forfeits derived from a first century work of Petronius where a boy climbed on the back of Trimalchio and called out, "Bucca, bucca, quot sint hic?"

Early Egyptians played Blindman's Bluff. The ancient Greeks called it Brazen Fly. The German version is Blind-Cow, the Spanish, Blind Hen. A Fourteenth Century treatise described ladies playing it. Adults continued to play it in the Seventeenth Century when Shakespeare called it Hoodman-Blind.

Parlor games and group activities diminished in the Twentieth Century when radio, television, and computers made home entertainment a solitary affair pairing the child or adult with a machine. However, the tremendous value to individuals and family of playing these games make it well worth the effort to revive them. Some of the values of playing games together are complying with rules, social interaction, verbal, math, and motor skills, self reliance, cooperation, and self acceptance based on group acceptance, not to mention the opportunity for creativity, ingenuity, and simple fun.

Successful Game Playing Is No Accident

Though this heritage of family game-playing is well established in the Gray family, it didn't happen by accident. Our parents, Chester and Pearl Gray, avid game players themselves, started the tradition in the family with Miriam and Harold, the first of their eight children. The rest of us have just continued their leadership even into the electronic age. Our parents were leaders in community parties at a rural church building close to The Wayside near Nevada, Missouri.

In a glassed-in bookcase in the living room, we recently found some old books of games dated from the turn of the Twentieth Century that our father had given our mother as gifts. Priceless to us are the notes in the margins in our parents' handwriting that told how they had adapted these games for specific gatherings. Turned-down corners indicated their favorite games.

These hints of advance preparation show one reason our parents were so successful in making game-playing enjoyable. They had experience with the game before they introduced it to a family or community group. Often they merely talked about it with each other to be sure they understood all the rules and had any needed equipment or supplies. Other times they played a practice game to be sure that the game really did suit the group. Miriam remembered that people in the community respected their leadership.

Now since the family has played the games

and become familiar with them for several generations, we need very little advance preparation to get one started. A word or two is all it takes.

Games that are family favorites include players of all ages and physical conditions. From the swing in the shade of the old elm tree at The Wayside, less active adults enjoy watching some of the outside running and hiding games that the younger ones play. We include the youngest members in some of the more complicated games by making them partners with older players and giving them some simple responsibility, such as passing out materials or simply announcing, "We're ready."

When our father's job took him to Washington, D.C., the family continued playing games in the new setting that included different friends. During the three to four days on the yearly trips back and forth to spend the summer on the Missouri farm, we passed the long hours in the car playing games. Eight or nine of us were crammed into one blue, 1929 Buick, with our luggage strapped on the running board. It was more than cosy with three in the front, three in the back with Carolyn on someone's lap, and Vernon and Ellen shoving each other from camp stools between the seats. Mama was inventive about ways to keep everyone happy. Games were the ideal solution.

Each of the eight siblings has continued the game-playing tradition in their individual families. Whether on the road or when we visit one another at our frequent family gatherings, games are often the order of the day.

Ingredients of Good Family Games

Good family game-playing minimizes winners and losers and finds ways to equalize the teams and players so that each member has an opportunity to participate at some level. We never worry about prizes or keeping prolonged scores because the main benefit of the games is the fun of playing.

The opportunity to see Vernon, a NASA scientist, lying on his back and kicking up his feet in the throes of death during a game of Killer is enough reward for any little sister. That same big brother can also enjoy seeing how really smart and quick his little sis is when they are on the same team in a game of Charades. Games are a leveling agent in the family because each person has different gifts and can show those talents when playing a variety of different games.

The most successful periods of game-playing

will include several types of games varying from the more intellectual to the just plain silly ones. A room full of distinguished adults can be reduced to tears of laugher by each in turn asking the one next to them, "Is Mrs. Mumbles home?" They must ask this without showing their teeth and without laughing or they are "out." The next in line answers, "I don't know. I'll have to ask my neighbor." Since everyone but the questioner and the answerer at that moment can laugh, this game becomes hilarious. When playing recently, the group almost broke up when five-year-old Marilyn answered, "No, she went somewhere else." She wasn't quite sure why everyone laughed so hard at her answer, but she certainly enjoyed being the center of attention for a few minutes.

Settings for Playing Games

Though many games work better if players sit in a circle, we don't let a lack of space hinder us. We can enjoy lively games of Murder and Coffeepot in motel rooms at night when two of our families happened to be traveling together. But the setting does need to be appropriate to the game and the people playing it. For example, a small group could play any guessing game in a car, a small room, or even in an intimate circle in a large hall. Obviously, the group would have to postpone active games for an outdoor setting. The important factor is to find a game that can be played in the available setting.

Leadership in Game Playing

Leadership, even in impromptu family games, is essential. The leader should be low key and lead by suggestions, not orders. He shouldn't approach a game like Kathryn, the big sister majoring in home economics, who used to order Carolyn, "Eat those Brussel sprouts. They're good for you." Games aren't fun and spontaneous if the leader says, "Everyone shut up and listen. I'm going to teach you a game." Invariably, groans follow that approach. A better way is to say enthusiastically, "Hey, guys, I know a fun game."

Although each family has its own pecking order for most things, that order doesn't have to decide the leadership role in game-playing. A new game suggested by an usually quiet relative can end up being the hit of the day.

Beginning with eager players, game leaders keep up the enthusiasm. Before starting, they make certain that everyone knows the rules.

Nothing can ruin a game quicker than people getting angry because they didn't know what to do or they didn't understand the object of the game. This problem can happen easily when a new in-law or a younger child becomes part of the group.

The temptation is to say, "You'll catch on after we start playing it." That makes the newcomer feel left out. Since the purpose of family games is to make everyone a part of the group, leaders need to be sensitive to any possibilities of hurt feelings.

The leader also needs to be aware of possible embarrassment. Games that use tricks and illusions can be successful and lots of fun as players try to figure out the solution, but they aren't much fun for the last one to catch on.

For instance, keen observers will enjoy the game, Black Magic, when they figure out that the word "black" is the clue in the question immediately before giving the correct answer. But the last one figuring out this solution may feel stupid and not enjoy the game.

The leader avoids unhappy players by making the clues more and more obvious as the game continues. For instance, as Miriam says the word, "black," she can stress it to point out that it is the clue in the game.

If Ellen is consistently the last one to catch on, then Miriam will ask her to be the knowledgeable partner on the next trick. She is now the one who knows the answers. If other players delight in tormenting the one who isn't quick in guessing, then it is time to change the game.

To avoid wearing out a game, leaders stop it while everyone still enjoys playing. One or two rounds of Poor Pussy can be great fun. The fourth or fifth time can get tiresome. Suggesting another game or ending the game-playing session for awhile keeps the group interested.

Equipment Needed

Since much family playing is spur of the moment, the most successful games are ones that require very little equipment--a rubber ball, a thimble, a ball of string, or objects available in most homes. Games that need more equipment or advance preparations are better saved for special events or planned parties as explained in Sections IV and V.

Choosing Sides

When a game needs two or more teams, successful leaders organize how the players choose sides so that certain people don't always get picked last.

Although they can ask the players to "count off," they can also find creative ways of forming teams that are as much fun as playing the game. They could ask players to line up without talking according to birth dates and then divide the line into the number of teams needed.

Or they might pre-determine the number of teams needed and select that many animals.

After whispering to players the name of an animal, the leader asks them to circulate, making the sound of that animal. As players listen for other meows or moos, they will find their teammates.

This method is particularly good when it is important to equalize the team for running or being a good guesser, for leaders can assign the teams without being overly obvious they are balancing them.

Another way uses animal names to randomly form the teams by having players draw the names of animals from a hat.

Other methods are the familiar "One potato, two potato...," "Eeny meeny miney mo," or "My mother said to choose this one" methods of pointing to each in turn in a circle. When the rhyme ends, that person joins the team.

Families That Play Together, Stay Together

Beyond the fun of the moment are the benefits of being with family members. Memories endure for years. Sharing those moments, that time of laughing, running, thinking, helps us to know one another better, makes each an important part of the group, and lets others value our gifts and talents. Playing games is a valuable family pastime for now and for posterity.

2

Fun for Everyone

Fun for Everyone

Let's all play. That's exactly what can happen in the games in this section of less active games. Grandparents and pre-schoolers (with some coaching) can all have fun.

Need special places? No. Crowded living rooms or outside under some trees will do. It doesn't matter.

Need much equipment? No. Hardly any at all.

On the spur of the moment when conversation dies down, or children get bored with all the talking about great aunts and uncles, Ellen may say, "I bet this group can't count to thirty in ten tries."

Naturally people disagree. "Of course we can," they say looking around at the group of educated adults and smart children. But they perk up knowing she's going to start a game.

"Not the way this game goes," Ellen says. "If

anyone makes a mistake, the whole group has to start back at one." She starts the counting and explains the special hand motions players must make instead of saying the numbers four and seven.

And, you know what? No group that's ever played that game with her has reached thirty! Even when they beg to have more than ten attempts. (See page 62 for complete directions.)

Before that game becomes tiresome, Carolyn will throw a sofa pillow at Mark saying, "My ship comes sailing." Mark, who knows the game, asks, "What is it carrying?"

"Cauliflower," Carolyn answers.

Mark throws the pillow to Brent, who just married into the family. After repeating the beginning words, Mark says his ship is carrying money. Brent has to figure out what the trick is and that his ship can't carry just anything. He must choose his cargo correctly or his ship will sink. But he isn't out if he chooses wrong. He watches and listens and when he gets another chance to sail his ship, with broad hints from others, he will choose something, like bicycles, an object beginning with the letter of his first name.

Soon Annie and Rosie may suggest Killer or Charades or Who's the Leader. The long afternoon evaporates into dinnertime while cousins, aunts, uncles, parents, and grandparents play together.

HOT POTATO
And Other Games That Eliminate Players One by One

This first sub-section of games finds the winner by eliminating players. But the best part is that those eliminated have as much fun as those still playing.

Hot Potato
Please Pass the Potatoes

A circle of players of any age and number quickly pass an object, which could be a real potato, a spool, or an orange, from one to another while someone plays music. The person left holding the 'potato' when the music stops is eliminated. The game continues until there only is the winner left.

Variation: To make the game seasonal and allow players to participate longer, pass a multiple-wrapped gift around the circle.

When the music stops, the holder of the gift removes as much wrapping as possible until the music begins again. The player is not eliminated, but passes the gift on. The one who removes the final wrapping is the winner and keeps the gift as a prize. In this variation players don't pass the "hot" object quickly but hold on to it as long as they can while unwrapping it. They want to see the prize and keep it.

To add to the fun and suspense, pass around several gifts either one at a time or all at once.

Killer
When a Friendly Wink Is Deadly

When a group plays Killer, players definitely remember the faces of each person in the group. During the game they constantly watch the eyes of those in the circle to identify the killer. This game is equally good with well-known friends and family or with those you have recently met. All that is needed is someone to take the initial leadership and a deck of cards.

Ann introduced this game several years ago. Since then it has been a perennial favorite with our family. When Lane and Beth attended their first reunion, they were planning to leave early, but when Lane became engrossed in Killer, they stayed late into the night enjoying the other games their cousins suggested.

The object of the game is to catch the murderer who kills by winking.

Killer needs from eight to twenty-five players of any age seated in a tight circle where they can see one another's eyes.

Without letting anyone else see their card, players select a card from a deck that contains the same number of cards as players. The one who draws the joker is the killer.

Quietly players, including the killer, glance around the circle into one another's eyes. When the killer thinks no one except his victim sees him, he winks. The wink "kills" the player, who must fall "dead" into the center of the circle. The victim can help by delaying death until the killer is looking away. Since he is dead, he cannot warn anyone else or give any clues. He stays there for the remainder of that round.

The game continues with the killer murdering players one by one until someone still "alive" spots him. Obviously the killer will not wink when he thinks someone is looking at him, but if Frances thinks she's spotted the killer, she calls out, "Judy, you're the killer." If Judy isn't the killer, then Frances is also dead and must fall into the center. If Judy is the killer, then that round of play is over. Pass out the cards for a new killer.

Hint: The leader can stack the deck for the first two or three times to allow someone to draw the joker who has either played the game before or will quickly understand the game. The leader will not give away the killer but continue watching the eyes around the circle as all other players do.

Variation: Often Miriam didn't want to fall to the floor, but slumped over in her chair to play dead.

On the other hand Ralph's death throes were the most effective. One time when Will killed him, he flopped to the floor, lay still for a second, then with his arms and legs in the air, twitched and writhed in dramatic anguish. Periodically, he would have another spasm, sending all of us into hysterics.

Musical Chairs
March until the Music Stops

This well-known children's favorite is also good with all ages. Place chairs either in a tight circle facing outward or in a row, each chair facing in the opposite direction from its neighbor. The players, one more than the number of chairs, march around the chairs as long as the music plays.

When the music stops, everyone scrambles for a seat. One person is left seatless and is eliminated from the game. After removing one chair, start the music again. Play continues until the winner claims the last seat in the last round of play.

Pig or Spoons
A Ridiculous Card Game

This game with two different names has similar goals but with slightly different rules. Carolyn has enjoyed this hilarious but competitive game with dignified professors and ministers who wanted a quick fun time between responsibilities. It is equally enjoyable with small children old enough to know their letters.

The equipment needed for Pig is a deck of cards. The Spoons version, in addition to the cards, needs one less spoon than the number of players. Three players or any number that can fit around a table can enjoy the game.

Deal four cards to each player with the extra cards

stacked by the dealer. The object is to be the first to get four matching cards, such as four eights or four queens. The dealer takes the cards one by one off of the unused portion of the deck, quickly looks to see if he wants it, and passes whichever card he doesn't want in his hand to the player on his right. She glances at the card and either passes it on or puts it in her hand and passes on another card. This action continues around the table with the last player stacking the discarded cards to the left of the dealer. If the deck is depleted before anyone has four like cards, the dealer starts over with the ones in the discard pile.

Pig

The excitement begins when someone has four alike. Carolyn is especially skilled in this part. In Pig, when she gets four matching cards, she quietly puts a finger beside her nose while continuing to pick up cards and pass them on so that no one notices her finger. When another player sees her finger beside her nose, that player immediately puts up a finger. The last one to notice the movement becomes a P.

The game continues with a new dealer until some unfortunate player has earned a P, an I, and finally a G. Once the player is a full-fledged PIG, the fun intensifies. In the Gray family our rule is that he is out of the game, but if he can get any other player to talk to him, that player also becomes a PIG.

Spoons

The game Spoons begins the same way with passing the cards around the table. The end is different. Put one less spoon than players in the middle of the table. The one who has four matching cards grabs a spoon. The scramble then begins as each player tries to get one of the remaining spoons. In this version, instead of spelling PIG to determine the loser, spell the word SPOON one letter at a time.

We suggest not using the family heirloom silver for this game. However, plastic spoons are not durable enough to withstand the competition.

When playing with small children, Carolyn prefers the PIG version to avoid anyone getting hurt in the scramble for spoons.

The first dealer can set the pace for future rounds by quickly passing around the cards and getting the adrenaline flowing as everyone frantically sorts cards, keeps only four cards in hand, watches other players' motions, and laughs with those who are slow to find their noses or grab a spoon.

Often the game doesn't have a real winner because players are so excited they forget to keep score and instead they play each round for the fun of the moment.

Sounds silly? That's the fun of it. We all need to be silly sometimes, no matter what our age.

This Is My Nose
And Other Games of Follow the Leader

The games in this section are quick, easily taught activities that are excellent for creating a good mood in either large or small gatherings. They can calm a group of school children or give needed comic relief to a group of men and women who have been in meetings all morning. These games require any number of players of any age who must follow the leader's actions and words in some manner. However, the fun is that players must be very alert and pay attention to the rules. Sometimes that means to follow the leader's instructions exactly and other times to do just the opposite. In Johnny, Johnny, Whoops Johnny, players become so focused on imitating the leader's finger actions and the unusual sequence of his words that they do not notice that he folds his arms at the end.

In several of the games, such as Birds Fly and Stand Up Sit Down, players must do the opposite of what the leader says or does.

When players make mistakes, they must either sit down or become the next IT. In Birds Fly and Simon Says, winners are often rewarded by becoming the next leader.

This Is My Nose
Confusing Body Language

With a very clear explanation before starting, this game is good with almost any number of people of at least grade school age.

Players stand in a circle with IT in the center. IT approaches any player and while holding his own elbow, says quickly, "This is my nose." That player must quickly put her hand on her nose and say, "This is my elbow." If she doesn't respond correctly or takes longer than the count of five, she becomes IT. If she is correct, IT must chose another victim and two other body parts to confuse. IT might then put his hand on his hip saying, "This is my foot." This mixes up the player more easily for when the counting is over, the player may have trouble figuring out how to hold a foot while saying, "This is my hip."

Depending on the agility and age of the players, some interesting contortions can develop.

The game continues until the leader calls time. It is important for the leader to see that everyone in the circle participates. Sometimes leaders play it by going around the circle, but that takes away the element of surprise because players know when their turn is coming. In a small group, the leader could go from one to another in turn, and then change to suddenly confront a player across the circle from the last "victim," insuring that everyone has a chance to play.

Variation: This Is My Nose is a good elimination game with the leader facing the whole group who reacts together. Anyone who makes a mistake must sit down.

Stand Up, Sit Down
Do As I Say, Not As I Do

IT sits in a chair in front of a seated group. The object is to catch a player making a mistake. Players must do as IT says, not as he does. He calls out either "Stand up" or "Sit down" in quick succession, sometimes making the action the same as his words, and sometimes not.

If he stands up while saying, "Sit down," players should remain seated. The first player to make a mistake becomes IT.

Hint: The leader should make sure that the new IT knows the game and is a good sport.

Donkey and Fiddler
Which One Are You?

The object of the game is to do the opposite of IT.

IT approaches a player and pantomimes playing a fiddle. While IT is doing that, the player puts her thumbs to her ears and wiggles her hands in imitation of a donkey. IT then faces another player, puts his thumb in his ears and wiggles his hands. That player must start the fiddler motion.

If the player does the wrong action, he becomes

IT. IT will change quickly from the fiddler action to the donkey as he goes from player to player, trying to catch someone.

Stick 'Em Up
Or You're Out!

In the middle of the circle of players, IT points to someone and says, "Stick 'em up."

That player must put both hands over his ears. The player on his right must put her left hand over her own left ear while the player on the left puts his right hand over his right ear. If any of the three make a mistake before IT counts to ten, the player making the mistake becomes IT.

Shifting Gears
But Not in a Car!

IT stands in front of the group with his right hand on his nose and his left hand on his right ear. All players imitate him. When IT calls "Shift," everyone puts the left hand on the nose and the right hand on the left ear. IT should call "Shift" rapidly to catch a player, who then becomes IT.

Variation: To make the shift harder, ask everyone to clap hands between each shift. Or to make it more of a rhythm activity, clap hands, then hit the knees between each shift.

Jericho and Jerusalem
To Bend or Not to Bend

With this game and the succeeding

ones, the last person left standing, the one who made no mistakes, is rewarded by becoming the next leader.

Players stand facing the leader. When the leader calls "Jerusalem," all players bend their knees. When he calls "Jericho," all stand still. Players must do what the leader says, not as he does. To confuse the players, the leader could bend his knees and call, "Jericho." When players bend their knees at the wrong time or do not bend when they should, they sit down. The last to sit down is the winner and can be the leader on the next round.

Birds Fly
Spread Your Wings and Fly

Like Jerusalem and Jericho, Birds Fly requires players to listen to what the leader says, not what he does. Facing the group of standing players, the leader calls out the name of something that does or doesn't fly and waves his arms if he wants to. Players, however, wave their arms only when the object mentioned does fly. While waving his arms, the leader might say, "Airplanes fly." Players should wave their arms. Next in rapid order the leader might say while waving his arms, "Bees fly;

houses fly." Since houses do not fly, players who wave their arms sit down. The winner is the one who makes no mistakes and is the last left standing.

Simon Says
Listen to Simon

"Simon says scratch your head," the leader, Simon, may say as he scratches his head. All players then follow Simon's instruction by scratching their heads. The leader repeats, "Simon says...," with different actions in quick succession while everyone follows him. But if he says, "Wipe your mouth," or some other action without saying first, "Simon says," players should do nothing. Those who do wipe their mouths must sit down.

Johnny, Johnny
Whoops, You Don't Get It!

This game of observation and memory played with two people or a large group is fun while traveling, sitting at home, or in a more formal setting as an ice-breaker or time filler. At an Elderhostel, Carolyn led this game with college professors, retired doctors, homemakers, and other professional people. It was fun to watch the earnestness with which all players followed directions and joined in the game.

The leader asks the group to watch carefully what she does and then repeat the exact actions and words when she finishes. She holds up her left hand with fingers spread apart. With the right index finger, she starts with the little finger and taps the tops of each finger saying, "Johnny, Johnny, Johnny, Johnny," one Johnny for each finger. When reaching the index finger, she runs her right finger down its side and up to the thumb tip saying, "Whoops, Johnny."

Then retracing her actions, she hits the thumb tip again, slides up the index finger saying, "Johnny, Whoops, Johnny," and continues with "Johnny, Johnny, Johnny," as she taps the tip of each finger on the way back.

The finger action and words are what the players watch carefully to imitate with the correct number of "Johnnys" and "Whoops." However the real trick is when the leader finishes the last "Johnny." She then casually folds her arms across her chest. Players, so intent on getting the "Johnnys" straight, rarely notice that action. They keep trying.

Facing the group, the leader can see if people do it correctly. She repeats and asks them to try again. As people try again to correctly follow the pattern, the leader will exaggerate crossing her arms until everyone finally sees what they missed.

There are no winners or losers, just a lot of good laughs from players who are sure they follow every movement.

Hint: Don't let this continue too long or let anyone feel embarrassed by not catching on. Bring those who have mastered the movement up front to join the leader. Seeing several crossing their arms in unison will usually be all that it takes for all the rest to catch on. Then they can plan how they can confuse others with the game at some other time.

Mrs. Mumbles
And Games Requiring Player Skills

This sub-section of games requires some skill from the players. The players must be observant in Who's the Leader and Ring on a String. They must do elementary figuring quickly in Count to Thirty, and do several actions at once in Widow Jones. Hardest of all, they must refrain from laughing in Poor Pussy.

Mrs. Mumbles
A Neighborly Game

When the family and guests are sitting in the

living room, Shirley likes to introduce a game she learned while helping with the church youth group. She turns to the one sitting next to her and without showing her teeth asks, "Is Mrs. Mumbles home?" Her neighbor answers, also without showing any teeth, "I don't know. I'll have to ask my neighbor." The neighbor turns to the next person and repeats the question. The questions and answers go around the room.

An additional stipulation to not showing any teeth is that neither of the speakers can laugh, or they are out. Everyone else in the room is usually roaring and watching the funny faces of those whose turns it is speak without showing any teeth.

Though it is a game of elimination, it doesn't take many turns around the room before everyone is either out or exhausted from laughter.

When Jim, who has an ample beard, seriously asked Claire the question, the movements of his beard and mustache broke up the game almost before it began.

However, he did not crack a smile (or if he did, we couldn't see it in his whiskers.)

No one has ever located Mrs. Mumbles.

Widow Jones
"She Died Last Night..."

This game provides much merriment as players laugh at one another as they continue the added-on actions of the leader.

No more than eight players of any age sit in a circle. The leader starts words and actions as other players in turn imitate him, not stopping the actions as the patter and actions go around the circle. At each new round, the leader adds a new action to the ones he continues to do.

For the first round, the leader says, "The Widow Jones died last night."

The first player asks, "How'd she die?"

"Going like this." The leader lifts his right leg up and down and continues that motion to the end of the game.

The first player then turns to the next player and repeats the words and actions. This dialog and action continues with each player until the last player is pumping his right leg up and down as are all of the other players.

In the next round the leader adds moving his left leg up and down as the players in turn pass the information around the circle.

Rounds three and four continue with patting the right hand on the right knee and the left hand on the left knee. For the last round, the leader nods his head.

By then everyone is laughing and worn out by all the foot and hand tapping.

Hint: If the group is large, divide the players into smaller groups. Too many players take too long to go through with the different rounds. A less active version with appropriate facial expressions and actions is: 1. With one shut eye; 2. With one shut eye and mouth awry; 3. With one shut eye and mouth awry and foot on high; 4. With one shut eye and mouth awry, and foot on high, and waving bye-bye. Continue with appropriate actions until the last player has had a turn and everyone ends waving bye-bye.

Poor Pussy
Try Not to Laugh

Any number of players of any age can play Poor Pussy anywhere.

The players try to keep from laughing at IT who is the Pussy.

The group sitting in a circle selects someone to be the Pussy. Pussy moves from player to player meowing, purring, or otherwise imitating a cat. Each player, without laughing, must pet Pussy while saying, "Poor Pussy," the three times she meows. If Pussy can't make a player laugh, she moves to another player. However, any player who laughs, becomes the next Pussy. The game continues.

Hint: It is usually easy to make people

laugh. Pussy can crawl, rub up against legs, yowl, scratch, or do any motions or sounds characteristic of cats. Carolyn even crawled up into poker-faced Vernon's lap and kneaded her fingers into his shirt. He laughed.

Gossip
Did You Hear What I Heard?

Any number of people of any age may enjoy this game together.

As the players are seated in a circle or around a table, one person whispers a phrase into the ear of a neighbor who in turn says the same thing into the ear of the next in line. Players can say the phrase only once. The listener tries to remember exactly what was said in order to repeat it accurately to the next in line.

At the end of the circle, the last player says aloud what he heard. The leader tells what the original phrase was. It is rare that the words remain the same throughout the game.

At a family reunion years ago when all but Ralph's car had reached the restaurant, we started the game of gossip to keep the children (and adults) from getting restless while waiting. Time passed quickly as we were engrossed in the game.

Count to Thirty
Group Cooperation Game

"I bet this group can't count to thirty." Ellen filled the pause in the conversation of a dozen people sitting in the living room.

Kevin, recent graduate in mining engineering, scoffed, "Anyone can count to thirty. I'll take you on."

"Okay, but you have to dry dishes if you lose."

Kevin smiled, confident that he had a sure thing.

That was all Ellen needed to challenge the group.

The object of Count to Thirty is simple. Without making a mistake, a group of people in a circle must reach thirty, counting one number to a player. But there are complications in the counting; it isn't just straight counting. It takes total concentration on the counting and team work. After every mistake, there is the challenge that the group can do it right the next time.

The ideal number of players is seven to thirty. Any age from third grade up can participate.

The leader begins the count. In turn, players number off. When the count reaches four, a multiple of four (8, 12, etc.) or a number with a four in it (14, 24), instead of saying the number aloud, the player claps his hands. The next one in turn then continues the count with five.

But that isn't all. When the count reaches seven or a multiple of seven (14, 21, etc.) or a number with a seven in it (17, 27), instead of saying that number out loud, the player hits the backs of his hands together. The next player continues the count aloud with the next number.

When anyone makes a mistake such as saying the number aloud, clapping wrong, or not paying attention to the sequence, the counting starts over with the next player. No one can give hints, for helping counts as a mistake.

Hint: After giving the instructions, don't warn players of traps such as numbers that contain elements of both four and seven such as fourteen and twenty-eight. Most players make a mistake here as they should clap both their palms and the backs of their hands. Over-confidence, like Kevin's, adds to the fun.

Variation: To make the game harder, instead of clapping the hands, for the number four make a hand movement under the chin pointing either right or left. For seven make the movement over the head. The way the hands point can change the direction of the counting, sending the turn back to the player on the left or forward to the next player.

After about fifteen tries, Ellen suggested another game. Kelly handed Kevin a dish towel.

Numbered Chairs
Number Please

Chair number one is the desired chair. As the game progresses, players try to reach that chair and remain there.

Ten or more people can play this game anywhere they can sit down. Children need to be old enough to count as high as the number of people playing.

Sitting in a circle, players number off counter-clock-wise. The number does not belong to the person but to the chair he is sitting in. The player in the highest numbered chair begins by calling out his number and some other number. "Twenty-one calling four."

"Four" must respond immediately by repeating his own number and calling another number. "Four calling six." The round continues until someone fails to answer quickly enough, speaks out of turn, calls a number not in the group, or otherwise makes a mistake. Then that person moves to the dummy seat (number twenty-one in this example), and all players between him and the dummy seat move one seat closer to one. The players who move now have a new seat number.

The game continues with much changing of seats and with everyone trying to oust those in low-numbered chairs.

Hint: It is fun to gang up on Number One by everyone calling that number. Before many times, the player will invariably make a mistake. Then everyone moves as Number One moves to the dummy seat.

Who Is the Leader?
IT Must Be Observant

IT must discover who is leading the group. Eight or more players of any age sit in a circle. IT leaves the room while the players select a leader. Before they call IT back into the room, the leader starts some action, such as patting his left foot on the floor, scratching his right ear, or clapping his hands. The others do exactly what he does. IT tries to pick out the leader who frequently changes the action. When IT spots the leader, a new IT leaves the room for another round.

Hint: The leader should not change movements while IT is looking his way. The more changes the leader makes, the more fun all will have. Nor should the players all watch the leader to point him out. They can look at another player to respond quickly to the change of actions.

Ring on a String
Another Challenge for IT

This game needs a length of string and a ring. IT must detect who has the ring.

Eight or more players of any age stand side by side in a circle. In their hands, they hold a string circling the entire group.

On the string is a ring which the players pass surreptitiously from one to another. IT stands in the center and tries to spot who has the ring. If successful, the person who has the ring becomes the next IT.

Hint: With palms down and hands holding the string lightly, players move their hands back and forth touching the hands of the people on either side. They can slip the ring under the hands to the next person and from hand to hand without IT spotting the ring. Other players can fake moving an imaginary ring to fool IT.

Murder
And Other Guessing Games

Guessing games have received a bad reputation in some circles because players are afraid they will look stupid if they can't come up with the answers. These games have enough action and fun built into them that no one needs to be put on the spot if unable to come up with the answers right away. In fact, Murder, Coffeepot, and I've Got A Bright Idea, require only one person to do the guessing. The others can enjoy watching IT try to figure out the answer from their clues.

Our family enjoys guessing games because all ages can join in, especially if the younger ones get some extra help and clues. Our time spent on the road gave us ample time to sharpen our skills by playing many of these games in the car.

The best thing about this group of games is that they can start spontaneously in almost any setting. Murder requires a darkened room and a deck of cards, but the others can begin at a moment's notice anywhere — in the car, on a lawn, in a living room. Well, Charades would be pretty hard in a car, but it probably could be done. So, I've Got a Bright Idea. Why don't we get together and play some guessing games?

Murder
A Crime to Solve

Murder was a favorite game when all of the Gray siblings were still home. Some cousins or friends visiting at night was all it took for someone to say, "Let's play Murder."

Any age or number that can easily move around in a room can play. It must be at night for the room needs to be dark. All that is need-

ed is a deck of cards or some other means of selecting the murderer and the detective. After the murder has occurred, the detective must find the murderer by asking questions and looking at the evidence.

Players select cards from those the leader holds. He should have the same number of cards as players. One specified card (joker, perhaps) is for the murderer, and another (king) is for the detective. Players then return the cards face down without anyone knowing which cards they drew, except for the detective, who acknowledges who he is. The detective turns out all the lights when leaving the room. It is more fun to be in as deep a darkness as possible.

Players then move around, though no one can leave the room. As murderer, Michael always takes his time to pick his time and his victim. He puts his hands around the victim's neck as if strangling her. She screams, yells, or makes whatever noises she wants and falls down "dead." The detective returns immediately on hearing the scream and switches on the lights. When the lights go on, everyone freezes in place.

The victim, of course, cannot say anything because she is dead. She stays where she fell after being murdered. The detective then surveys the scene, asks questions of everyone, trying however he can to find out who did it. All players must answer truthfully, except the murderer. He can lie all he wants. The others will help the detective but only by answering questions. They cannot offer information without being asked.

When the detective solves the crime, the cards are passed again, and the game continues with a new detective and a new murderer.

Hint: Small children can play, though the leader should make sure they do not get the card for detective. If the detective isn't old enough to ask the right questions, the game will lag. Instead of random card selections, the leader can whisper to each player, thus choosing a good player to be the detective.

One time when the lights came on, we found Papa climbing on our upright piano. He had one foot on the piano bench, the other on the end of the keyboard, and his hands on top of the piano. It turned out he was the murderer, and he was attempting to get an alibi by being far from the murder scene when the detective returned.

Coffeepot and Teakettle
Non-caffeinated Fun

These two games are so similar that it is hard to choose one over the other. Any place is suitable for either as long as everyone can hear. One player leaves the room (or if in a car, he covers his ears) while the group decides on an action phrase for Coffeepot or an object for Teakettle. An action phrase might be, "to wash the dishes" or "to ski." An object can be anything like a painting or a car. To get more difficult, it can be Van Gogh's "Sunflowers" or a Model T Ford.

If Ralph is the guesser, he returns and by asking questions that can be answered only by yes or no, tries to figure out what the phrase or word is. When asking the questions, he substitutes the words coffeepot or teakettle for the unknown word. So he might ask Donna, "Have you coffee potted in the last week?"

If the phrase is "to eat a tomato" for example, Donna answers, "Yes, I have Coffee potted."

Ralph then might ask Heather, "Have I ever seen you coffeepot?" The hidden meanings in some innocent questions add to the fun. When Ralph guesses the correct phrase, the person

71

who was the one to give it away takes the turn as guesser.

Teakettle uses the same routine, except the questions might be, "Can I see a teakettle now?" "No." Or, "Do we have a teakettle in our bedroom?" The guesser's train of thought can vary widely from the chosen words, adding to the fun as players see that the guesser is on the wrong track.

Hint: Our family plays the game often enough that no one has trouble asking proper questions. However, if the game is new to the group, be sure that the first guesser is someone who can quickly come up with good questions.

Variation: Sometimes the rule is to ask each individual only three questions before moving on to the next person. It is hard sometimes not to follow up on a hunch from one person's answer when a series of questions to the same person can find the answer.

I Am Somebody
But You Must Find Out Who

This game is good almost anywhere. It passes away many tedious hours traveling in a car.

Two or more players of any age can play. They try to figure out by asking questions who that Somebody is.

The Somebody can be real or fictional or a specific animal, such as the family dog. One player thinks of a person, for instance, Abraham Lincoln. Then she says, "I am Somebody." Other players ask questions that can be answered only by yes or no, such as: "Are you a man?" "Yes." "Are you famous?" "Yes." "Are you dead?" "Yes." "Were you a relative?" "No." "Were you a president?" And so forth until a player calls out the correct name.

The player who first calls out the correct name gets to be Somebody next.

Hint: Even little children can play if occasionally the answer is someone they know, like Daddy or Santa Claus.

Variation: Expanding the game to "I am something," opens up a much larger range and makes guessing harder.

Wordy Guessing Games

The next four games require players to use their word skills and ingenuity. The leader selects something that the others must guess. In these games the leader gives them some clue to begin. All of these games are good on car trips.

I've Got a Bright Idea
How's It Like Me?

When the leader picks an object, she says, "I've got a bright idea." Let's say she selected a lamp. Any player can ask, "How's it like me?"

The leader then uses her ingenuity to come up with comparisons to the player that asked but not enough to give it away right off.

For instance, if Sandy asked that question, the leader might say, "It is tall." Or if Jeff asked, the answer might be, "It is bright." Whoever guesses the identity of the object is the leader of the next round.

Hint: If any of the bright ideas become offensive, it is time to change the game.

Variation: Instead of the leader selecting the object, the players chose an object while the leader is out of the room. Then the players give clues about the object comparing it to the leader. There is no special order, but any player can give a clue.

I'm Thinking of Something That Rhymes With
Rhyme Time

When the leader chooses some object, he begins, "I'm thinking of something that rhymes with [for example] rug." A player, instead of blurting out an answer, may ask, "Is it something you drink out of?" The leader has to figure out what word the player means. "No," the leader says, "It's not a mug." "Is it a big fellow?" another asks. "No, it is not a lug." "Is it an insect?" "No, it is not a bug."

Players continue asking until one guesses the correct word, "jug." That player becomes the next leader.

Variation: For small children, the unknown could be, "I'm thinking of something that is green," or "starts with A." It can be a person (I'm thinking of some person that rhymes with...) Or "I see something that rhymes with..." Depending on the players, there are lots of possibilities.

Fat Cat
Rhymed Definitions

In this game anyone can begin. There are

no winners or losers nor any real structure. Playing it passes the time on car trips and provides any group with quiet interaction and mental stimulation. Someone may ask, "What is a corpulent feline?" Whoever thinks of the answer first, says, "A fat cat."

The answer is two words, an adjective and a noun that rhyme. The question gives synonyms of each of the words. Some examples are: Pregnant reptile (fertile turtle); distant automobile (far car); a chic woman (classy lassie).

Charades
Modern Versions of an Historic Game

Charades is an age-old game with many variations. Though books of parlor games in the late 1800s give directions for Charades, historical mentions of it date even further back. In the original game, one person acted out one word for the others in the group to guess. That person could use no words or sounds, communicating only through gestures and actions. An example of this type of charades is an unmarried woman or girl sitting underneath a small table. The word acted out was Misunderstand.

In the 1930s, Charades developed into a team

game--acting out phrases, titles, or personalities. Entitled simply THE GAME the action followed these rules: Two teams go into different rooms where they cannot see or hear one another. A leader stands between the two teams with a list of ten things she has worked up for the others to act out. She has composed a list of similar subjects, such as titles, animals, places, or miscellaneous things. She notifies the players what the category is before the play begins. One person from each team comes to the leader to read silently the first item on the list. Then they hurry back to his team to act out what they read. The team member who guesses correctly, hurries to the leader to see the next item on the list. The team that goes through the list of ten the quickest wins that round.

Hint: The leader has to be careful to show only the next item as the players rush in. One way for the leader to avoid mistakes is to have the player tell what his correct guess was. Another is to use a blank piece of paper to hide the following items on the list.

Variation: Another way to play this same game is to have both teams in the same room. Before the game begins, each team composes a list of several items. Each player on the team then comes, in turn to the opposing team, to be assigned a word, phrase, or title to act out. Someone keeps track of the amount of time needed to guess the word. The team using the least time wins. The advantage of this variation is that everyone enjoys seeing the acting of the entire group, and everyone can choose what will be acted out. Instead of one team going through the whole list at once, the actions can alternate between sides while still having a timekeeper.

Hint: There are some standard motions that aid in the acting. Some examples are pretending to sing for song titles, acting as if holding a book for the title of a book, or making a square in the air for a television program. To help in the number of words, simply hold up fingers to indicate total number and then fingers to indicate which word is being acted out.

Variation: This same game can be replicated by using a newsprint tablet. The clues are drawn on the paper instead of acted out. The play continues as in the earlier versions except that players giving the clues use markers and paper instead of body language. They cannot write letters.

This version was popular in a television game called "Win, Lose, or Draw" and also resulted in a commercial board game of "Pictionary." It can be just as much fun without the commercial props.

Small children can play any of these variations either to help guess or, with a little coaching, to act out an item. In our family, we always bend the rules a bit so we can include the little ones at whatever level they can participate.

Our Minister's Cat
And Other Memory Word Games

Testing memory and word knowledge can turn out to be very entertaining when done in the following games. When players are creative in the attributes of that poor cat in the parsonage, or in their choice of what to "take to New York," the fun multiplies. Once after Our Minister's Cat was described as awful, bad, and cute, Kathryn suggested that he was also declawed. Each time we reached that word we shared another laugh at her description.

Though Ghost is harder, trying to bluff others is also fun. When Ralph couldn't think of a letter that didn't end the word, he would suddenly "think" of such a letter and confidently add it to the list, not having the foggiest idea if it were a word. Trying to outguess the bluff or seeing how long a bluff could continue added to this more serious game.

Our Minister's Cat
A Brainy Challenge

Children old enough to know the alphabet can play this memory game.

Claire begins the game by saying, "Our minister's cat is awful," or any adjective that begins with A. Ann, her aunt who is the next player, repeats, "Our minister's cat is awful..." and then adds, "and beautiful," an adjective beginning with B. Other players in turn add, "cute, darling, and egotistical," or any descriptive word starting with the next letter of the alphabet after repeating what others said. A player who misses is eliminated. The game continues until there is a winner. After completing one alphabet, go through it again without repeating any word until there is only one player left.

When I Go to New York
Another Alphabet Game

Like Our Minister's Cat, When I Go To New York tests players' memory, but instead of adjectives, players list nouns (things) in alphabetic order.

The leader begins, "When I go to New

York, I'll take apples," or anything beginning with A. The next player repeats, "When I go to New York, I'll take apples," and adds something beginning with B, "and bananas."

The game continues until there is a winner as in Our Minister's Cat.

Ghost
A Game of Spelling, Strategy, and Entrapment

Good spellers are better at this game, but it is also fun for those of us who aren't. It is a spelling game that doesn't end when you're "out." When we are eliminated from the spelling part by completing three words and thus becoming a ghost, we can have lots of fun as we try to trick other players to join us as ghosts. Though our father was rarely the first one to become a ghost because he was very good at spelling and thinking of alternative endings to words, he was a master at entrapment. Maybe we'd better explain the game first, then we can show how the ghost part fits in.

Three to eight players are ideal for this game. It can be played in any setting but is an excellent game to play while traveling. The first player starts by saying a letter. Each player in turn adds another letter toward a real word until someone names a letter that finishes a word. The object is to avoid being the one that adds a letter that ends a word. Instead, the strategy is to add a letter that forces other players to end the word. For instance, if the letters so far were S-H-A-R, instead of adding E, which would end a word (share), add an I (thinking of sharing). If a player cannot add a letter without ending a word, or doesn't notice that the letter ends a word, that player becomes one-third of a ghost.

For example, Carolyn might start with a B. Next in line is Ellen who says O (thinking of BOY). Mama takes her turn by adding S (thinking of BOSS). Kathryn has a hard time thinking of something other than BOSS, because other words such as BOSSY will have the word BOSS within it and would therefore end a word. She does think of BOSOM, so she says O. Gertrude knows what word Kathryn has in mind but is unable to think of any other choice, so she adds M. She becomes one-third of a ghost. (Kathryn gets a stern look from Mama for bringing up such a personal word as bosom!)

Bluffing and challenging are options. If Ralph can't think of a letter that doesn't end a word, he can try bluffing by assuming a knowing look and saying another letter. This has consequences. Vernon, who is next in line, can then doubt that Ralph knew a word and say, "I challenge you." If Ralph did not have a real word in mind, then he becomes one third of a ghost. If he really knew a word, then Vernon, who challenged him, becomes one third of a ghost.

A round of spelling ends when a player becomes a third of a ghost. Another round begins with the next player starting a new word. A player who ends three words becomes a full ghost and cannot participate in the spelling. Then the fun intensifies as another level of the game begins. A ghost can talk to any of the players, but if players respond directly to a ghost, they immediately become a full ghost and cannot continue spelling. The game ends with only one live body in the ghostly group.

Hint: When players become ghosts, they can devise methods of trickery to get the spellers to speak to them. Papa could catch any of us. He seemed to lose interest in the game as he was attending to his driving, Then he would quietly ask a simple question like, "What time is it, Gertrude?" She would automatically answer and thus become a ghost.

In order to elicit a response, the younger kids sometimes become real pests by harassing others to get them to speak to them. We made a rule that ghosts could not touch those still playing. After all, since ghosts don't exist and can't be heard or spoken to, they cannot touch people.

Variation: We often play that two letter words, like DO or AT do not count as ending a word.

Hangman
Capital Punishment with Words

If several are playing, Hangman needs a blackboard or newsprint tablet. A piece of paper and a pencil is all that is necessary if only two or three are playing.

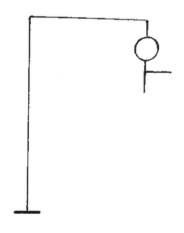

The leader draws a "gallows" and under it makes one mark for each letter in the word. As players guess a letter, the leader writes it on the proper blank line.

If the letter appears more than once in the word, print the letter only one time until someone guesses it again. However, if the letter guessed is not in the word, draw one body part under the noose of the gallows, starting with the head, the neck, the body, two arms and two legs. If no one guesses the word before the victim's body is completed, the leader wins. The hangman has a complete victim.

Usually then the leader erases the first word and the hung victim and starts another word. If a player fills in the blanks and completes the word before the hanging, that player chooses the next word.

Hint: It avoids confusion if the players guess in turn instead of at random.

Dictionary
Competing with Noah Webster

This is one of the few games in this collection that smaller children can't play. Teenagers and adults will enjoy matching wits in this vocabulary game.

Dudley introduced this game to the family many years ago. The leader looks in a good dictionary to find a word that he thinks no one knows. He asks the group to make sure. He writes the correct dictionary meaning on a piece of paper. In the meantime, each of the other players write on separate pieces of paper an imaginary definition of the word trying to make it sound as much like a real dictionary definition as possible. All definitions, including the real one, go into a container. The leader then reads each definition in turn, with individuals guessing which is the correct one.

Those guessing correctly gain a point, and the player whose fake definition got the most votes also gets a point. A new leader begins the second round.

Hint: Be sure to find a word no one knows. The leader should make the definition less bookish, while players can come up with long-winded definitions to make it more challenging.

Black Magic
And Other Tricks and Illusions

The following games allow the two people who know the trick or clue to amaze the others with their "powers." It is fun to play even if several others know the trick as long as there are newcomers in the group. Carolyn and Ellen do these trick games often at Elderhostel classes.

Carolyn leaves the room. While she is out the group selects an object. She returns and identifies what the group chose by clues Ellen gives her. The other players figure out what clues or signals Ellen gives that allow Carolyn to identify the chosen object. When a players thinks he knows the trick, he can leave the room to test his "skill."

It usually takes several times demonstrating until someone figures out the trick. A good leader won't let the game go on too long, but gives exaggerated clues or hints so everyone will catch on. The leader can emphasize or dramatize something that gives away the clue. For instance in Black Magic, Ellen can say, "Is it this black shoe?" with black being the clue. This emphasis helps players find the clue themselves. Since they feel smart if they figure it out, the leader will give hints. It's no fun if people feel stupid or left out.

Black Magic
A Dark Secret

The clue in Black Magic is the word black.

When the group selects an object in the room, the leader calls her partner back in. The leader walks around pointing to various objects. "Is it this chair?" "No," the partner replies. The leader continues pointing and asking until she points to something black. Then the partner shows his magic because the next thing the leader points to is the selected object.

Jamboree
Watch the Door for Clues

Jamboree is similar to Black Magic. The group selects an object and when the leader calls her partner back, she points to various objects and asks if that is the correct one. As in Black Magic, the clue to the magic is in the title of the game — the JAMB in Jamboree. When the partner leaves the room, he puts one to five fingers on the door jamb. Three fingers mean that the third object the leader points to is the article selected.

In Cahoots
Magical Communication

As in Black Magic and Jamboree, the partner leaves the room while the group chooses an object. When the partner returns, both the leader and partner notice which of the players speaks first. The leader then asks, "Are you in cahoots?" That means is the partner clear about who spoke first. If so, the partner says, "Yes." But if several people are talking at once, or it isn't definite who spoke, then the partner says, "No, not yet."

Then perhaps Sally says something to Julie. The leader asks again, "Now are you in cahoots?" "Yes." They both now know that Sally is the clue, and they are in cahoots.

The leader points to various objects asking in turn if this is what the group chose. In the question just before pointing to the correct object, the leader will mention Sally's name in some way. For instance, the leader may say, "Is it Sally's red blouse?" "No," but the partner is alerted to say yes to the next question which is the correct answer.

Hint: Since this clue is difficult for the players to recognize, the leader might make a big deal out of mentioning Sally's name. Or after a few trials when no one catches on, if David says something first, the leader can bring the group's attention to his name in some way. Then when the leader mentions David's name again while asking the question, players can see that David is the clue.

Concentration
Think Hard about This

In Concentration, after the partner leaves the room, the group decides on a number under ten. When the partner returns, she cups her hands on the faces and jaws of a few people and looks into their eyes, telling them that by mental telepathy she will learn the number. When she comes to the leader and places her hands on his face, he will work his jaws, like chewing gum, the correct number of times of the number selected.

Scissors Crossed
And So Are the Legs

Scissors Crossed needs a pair of scissors and any number of people sitting in a circle. The leader says, "There is a trick in the way I pass the scissors around the circle. See if you can see what it is." Then the leader passes the scissors to the right saying, "I pass these scissors crossed (or uncrossed)." He can leave them closed or opened without regard to what he says.

Most people will concentrate on the scissors and not notice that the leader crosses (or uncrosses) his legs according to what he says. The "crossing" or "uncrossing" has nothing to do with the scissors, only with his legs.

The scissors continue around the circle with each player saying the dialog. No one is eliminated, but the leader tells players whether they are right.

Hint: The partner and others who know the trick should be scattered around in the circle so that the game doesn't drag with player after player being wrong. To help people solve it, when the leader says, "I pass these scissors crossed," he can emphasize the word and at the same time very obviously cross his legs. The game ends when everyone catches on.

Tricks Using Five and Nine Books
Do You Get My Point?

These two games use books or magazines laid out on the floor or on a table where all players can see them. Lester and Carolyn enjoy this game. The group selects one of the books while Lester is out of the room. When he returns Carolyn points to various books asking if this is the one chosen. Since Lester knows the trick, he always gets it right.

Five Book Trick

In Five Book Trick, lay five books side by side in

one row. Carolyn will point to various books asking if this is the correct one. The trick is that she points to the selected book in accordance to its position as it is laid out — 1, 2, 3, 4, or 5. If the book chosen was number 3, then she will point to it on her third question.

Hint: Most people will think the trick has to do with something about the books themselves, not the number of their location. So don't mention numbers until you need to give hints to help them figure it out. Then you could ask, "Is it the third book?"

Nine Book Trick

In Nine Book Trick, like Five Book Trick, the clue is in the placement.

Place nine books in three rows of three books each making a square as in the illustration. After the group selects one of the books and Lester returns, Carolyn touches different books asking if it is the one. The trick is on her first question, she touches the cover of the book at the position that the chosen book is in the grid of nine books. For example, if the group chooses the center book, on her first question she touches the middle of any book (though not the selected book). Since she has given Lester the clue, she can point to other books in any order until she points to the middle one.

Variation: In this method, the clue isn't given in the first book touched. Carolyn points to one or two books that weren't selected. Then to identify the chosen book, she touches its cover in the spot that indicates its placement in the grid. For instance, to indicate the center book using this method, she points to the middle of the center book in the grid. When indicating the other books, she points any-place, but is careful not to touch the part of the cover that represents the book's position in the grid.

My Ship Comes Sailing
Your Name's the Clue

Anyone who can spell will enjoy this trick game played anywhere with something that can be tossed harmlessly like a ball or a pillow.

Seated in the circle of players, Laura begins by tossing a ball to Susan saying, "My ship comes sailing." Susan catches the ball and asks, "What is it carrying?" Laura answers, "Lemons," naming something that begins with the letter of her first name. She could have named something starting with G for her last name, Gray, but since this is family, too many people have the same last names. So she decides to use her first name this time.

Knowing the trick, Susan agrees that the ship will not sink carrying lemons. She then tosses the ball to Erick. She says her cargo is snakes, or to make it more interesting, she may say "slithering snakes."

Erick hasn't played the game. He says his ship carries cats. His ship sinks. He didn't add something beginning with E. However, he isn't out of the game which continues until all players catch on.

Hint: Toss the ball frequently to those who

know or soon catch on to the trick to give the others clues. Ellen is a good hint-giver by emphasizing the names. When her turn comes, she tosses the ball to Brian. When he asks what her ship is carrying, as if reminding herself of the various cargos, she says, "Laura said, lemons, Susan said slithering snakes, Alison said apples, Jim said jack-a-lanterns, Tom said tomatoes, Gavin said grapes, and I'll add eggplant."

Games of Illusion

The following eight games, or tricks, are fun when there are new people in the group who haven't played. Even if most players know the trick, there need be only one gullible person.

Broom and Water Trick
Try Not to Get All Wet

This trick needs a broom, a bowl or shallow pan, water, and a good-humored player. Fill the bowl half full of water. Place it against the ceiling and support it with the broom handle.

Then ask a player to hold the broom handle while everyone else leaves the room temporarily. The joke is on the player left holding the container of water against the ceiling because without help from someone else, there is no way that person can get the container down without spilling the water.

Penny on the Forehead
Is It There or Not?

The leader presses a penny that is body temperature on his own forehead to show that it will stay there. Then he firmly presses the coin onto the center of the forehead of another player but immediately removes it. The player can still feel the coin and thinks it is still there.

The object is for the player to remove the coin using only facial muscles. The fun is watching the exaggerated facial expressions while trying to remove the imaginary coin.

Nose Wriggling Contest
Make All the Faces You Want

All players lie on the floor, face up, looking at the ceiling. Balance a coin on the tip of each player's nose. When all the players and coins are in position, tell them there will be a race to see who is the first one to successfully wiggle the coin off the nose without moving any part of the body except facial muscles. It isn't fair to shake the head or blow. Any kind of facial gymnastics is permitted.

Going to Heaven On a Board
It Feels Like an Airplane Ride

This trick is played on one person at a time. Have other players who do not know the trick go into another room and wait their turn. The trick requires a board and some bricks or books to elevate the board three or four inches from the floor.

If we played this trick on Maria, we would blindfold her and ask her to step up onto the elevated board. It takes three other people to do the trick. The leader stands on the floor by Maria and puts a hand on her head or shoulder. He tells her she is going to heaven on a board. When the other two helpers slowly lift the board only a few inches, the leader squats to give Maria the sensation of being lifted high into the air. Then holding her hand to steady her, he asks her to jump off. She prepares for a big jump and is surprised to find she is only inches from the floor.

Variation: Instead of the leader squatting, when Maria is lifted up, he taps her on the head with a broom to give the sensation of hitting the ceiling.

String Hand Cuffs
No Fair Breaking the String

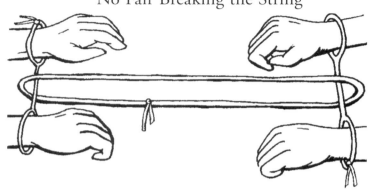

This game is effective as an ice-breaker or a contest to see which pair can first get loose. Tie the wrists of each player together as in handcuffs. Then pairing off, tie a string between two sets of handcuffs.

The players must figure out how to get apart without untying the knots or slipping their hands out of the handcuffs.

Hint: The trick is to slip the string holding the pair together under the string handcuff at one player's wrist and over the hand.

Though the players still have handcuffs, they are free from the partner.

Visual Illusions

The following three tricks which Dudley taught us will not only amaze your guests but are fun to do alone.

Making Arms Raise
Relax and Let Them Soar

Ask guests to stand in an open doorway and press the backs of both hands firmly against the two side casings.

They should exert outward pressure on the door casings for about fifteen seconds.

When they step out from the doorway, their arms will automatically rise.

Shorten Your Arm's Length
No, You Aren't Deformed

Stand an arm's length away from a wall and extend the right arm and hand, allowing only your fingertips to touch the wall.

Bend the arm back and rub the elbow with the other hand.

Then extend your right arm out again to the wall. Do not stretch the arm to touch the wall. This time the fingers will not touch the wall and the arm will appear shorter.

When the guests repeat the motions, their arms will also appear shorter because they unconsciously do not stretch out their arm the second time.

Pin in Arm
It Doesn't Hurt a Bit

First demonstrate the trick by holding your arm straight out in front of you. With the sharp point toward your shoulder, place a straight pin in the loose skin inside your arm at the elbow. Slowly bend your arm. The pin will appear to go through your skin, but it won't prick you because of the protective loose skin. Then ask the guests to do the trick.

Cows and Horses
And Other Car Games

While many of the quieter living room games in this book can be played in the car with adaptations, this sub-section, includes games that can be played only in a moving vehicle because an essential part of the game is what is passing outside. Obviously, someone cannot leave the room while you are driving down an interstate highway, but someone can close her eyes and put her hands over her ears to get the same results.

One advantage is that the travelers will actually look outside and not have their noses buried in an electronic game, thus missing the grandeur of the countryside.

Cows and Horses
Livestock Roundup

To begin the competitive game of Cows and Horses, divide the people in the vehicle down the middle, right and left. Then the teams watch on their side and count out loud the number of cows and horses they see. If only two people are playing, one on each side, they can count silently, which probably pleases the driver more.

The game ends at a pre-determined time or place. The side with the most animals wins.

Two rules add to the excitement of the game. Finding a white horse doubles the accumulated score. But passing a cemetery buries all the animals and that team must start over again. Our family added a third rule that a cat in a window adds one hundred points. Gertrude added this rule to keep the interest in the game while driving through towns.

This game is simple enough that any child who can count can be part of the team or can play against another person in the car. It is surprising how quickly the time passes when each turn of the road may bring a pasture full of animals.

There are some areas where this game is boring because there are no animals. In the mountains, along metro-sprawl or in cities you might select another game. Four-lane divided highways pose some fairness problems. Those who must look over two lanes of traffic to see a field are at a disadvantage. However, two-lane roads in the country still offer miles of fun with this game.

Roadside ABCs
Another Way to Get Your Zs

Players find each letter of the alphabet in its correct order by watching signs and billboards. Each person plays alone.

An obvious disadvantage to dividing into left and right teams is that players must turn around to read the signs on the left.

Also on interstate highways the signs on the left are farther away and more difficult to read. The person or team that finishes the alphabet first is the winner.

Players tell what letter they are on whenever asked so the others know how they rank.

As children get older, and to make the game more challenging, limit the letters to those at the beginning of words. Since words starting with Q and X are rare, this version lasts longer. Thank goodness for Dairy Queens! We sometimes eliminate the X words. Z isn't difficult to find in different types of zones.

License Plate ABCs

A similar game uses the letters on license plates.

In this version, players work individually, as you can't divide the sides of the road when driving down one side of it. Players go through the alphabet by finding the letters in sequence on different license plates on cars or other vehicles ahead of them, behind them, in the opposite lane, or even parked. When Les was eleven, he always beat the rest of us finding the right sequence of letters.

Another version of the License Plate game is to give lists of all fifty states to those in the car. Then see who can find every state before the end of the trip. Players could earn extra points for Alaska, Hawaii, and foreign countries. Those who find all might win some special prize.

Hide the Thimble
And Other Miscellaneous Games

The first game that most children in the Gray family learn is Hide the Thimble. Though Papa was a master at hiding the thimble in clever places, small children can be just as inventive. Very small children become part of the group playing if adults include Ring Around the Rosie and Mulberry Bush. The relay races we all remember from gym classes at school and children's parties can be as much fun for the older group if they are chosen wisely. Steal the Prize has become a favorite in a rural women's club near our family farm, for it involves everyone. Since the only skill needed is remembering who has won which prize, everyone has a great time laughing at the luck, or lack of it, in choosing "red or black."

What If should be saved for very special times in a close setting such as a car or a few people in a room. Any game helps people get to know one another a little better, but this one can really open doors. Speaking of doors, let's go inside and see who is ready to play with us.

Hide the Thimble
I Spy

We have never found a child who didn't enjoy playing Hide the Thimble. It is also fun for the adults who play along with the children to find ingenious places to hide the little thimble.

When everyone leaves the room, Kelly hides the thimble in plain sight when you look at it. The other players return to the room and begin looking. When Shirley sees the thimble, she moves to another part of the room before saying, "I spy," so the others won't know where she was when she spied the thimble. She sits down and watches the others who are still looking.

After a time Kelly will give clues by saying, "Shelbie is getting warmer," meaning Shelbie is near the thimble, "but Maria and Jordan are very cold," meaning Maria and Jordan are far away. As they move in response to these clues, Kelly might add, "Now Maria is getting warm, too, but Shelbie better watch out or she will burn!" Everyone moves near Shelbie. As players see the thimble, they say, "I spy," and sit down to watch the others hunt. The first one to spot it gets to hide it the next round.

Besides the room itself, non-participating adults in the room make good hiding places. Put the thimble on Deborah's finger or on the toe of John's shoe.

Hint: Pair up very small children with a partner so they can be part of the game.

Blind Man's Bluff
A Favorite Since Roman Days

Usually associated with children, Blind Man's Bluff has been popular with adults for centuries. In the center of a ring of players, the leader blindfolds a player and turns him around several times to make him lose his sense of direction. When the leader releases the Blind Man, he tries to find another player who cannot move from the circle. After Blind Man locates someone, he must identify that person by feeling for hair styles, glasses, or other features. If he guesses correctly the identified player takes a turn

in the center being blindfolded. If the Blind Man guesses wrong, he must find another person in the circle and try again. The game continues until all players have a chance to be the Blind Man.

Variation: The game can be a prelude to Forfeits (page 116). The identified person must pay a forfeit to be redeemed in the follow-up game of Forfeits. After the player has been identified, pays her forfeit, and takes her turn with the blindfold, she then drops out of the circle.

Ring Around the Rosie
And We All Fall Down

Small children enjoy the simple game of Ring Around the Rosie that has no winners or losers. If Grandpa joins in, it is even more fun. Everyone holds hands in a circle and moves counter clockwise while chanting the words, "Ring around the rosie, a pocket full of posies, ashes, ashes, we all fall down." At the words, "We all fall down," that's just what the children do--fall down amid their laughter.

Here We Go 'Round the Mullberry Bush
As We Go Through the Days of the Week

Similar to Ring Around the Rosie, the Mulberry Bush begins with children holding hands and circling in time to their singing. "Here we go 'round the mulberry bush, the mulberry bush, the mulberry bush. Here we go 'round the mulberry bush, so early in the morning."

At the end of the chorus, they sing a verse which they act out. "This is the way we wash our clothes, wash our clothes, wash our clothes. This is the way we wash our clothes early Monday morning." They pretend they are rubbing clothes on a washboard.

In between the next six verses they repeat the chorus.

"This is the way we iron our clothes." (Tuesday)

"This is the way we mend our clothes." (Wednesday)

Sweep our floor (Thursday), Make our bed (Friday), Shine our shoes (Saturday), and Go to Church (Sunday).

Hint: Since modern children may be puzzled at some of these daily tasks, the adult leader can substitute whatever she chooses, such as, "This is the way we make our bed; Vacuum the rug; or Load the dishwasher." Let the children choose the actions. Maybe they might even sing, "This is the way we order our pizza!"

Steal the Prize
Possession Is Ten/Tenths of the Law

Carolyn learned this game at a club meeting where twenty women were sitting in a living room. Any number of people of any age can play Steal the Prize in almost any setting. It is a simple game that requires a deck of cards and enough inexpensive and silly prizes for everyone there.

As leader, Carolyn asks each player in turn to guess whether the next card in the deck she holds in her hand is red or black. After the guess, she exposes the card. If the guess is wrong, the play moves on to the next person. If she guesses the right color, she may choose an unwrapped prize from the sack. After winning the prize, she puts it out of sight.

The game continues after all the prizes are distributed. Players who guess red or black correctly steal the prize that another player has previously won. However, they must remember who has the prize and what it is since the prizes are not in plain view.

For example, if Mary Ellen wins a change purse, and Ruth guesses the right color of card and wants the change purse Mary Ellen has already won, Ruth must say, "I want Mary Ellen's change purse." If Mary Ellen no longer has the change purse, since someone earlier stole it, then Ruth loses her chance at getting a prize on that round.

The leader determines when the game ends by announcing the last round of play. After all players have had one more chance to steal a prize, the game ends with those keeping whatever prizes they still have.

Variation: Stealing the desired prize is a fun way to distribute gifts when people bring presents to a Christmas party. Guests pick numbers from a container for their order of selecting. Number one chooses one of the wrapped gifts. She unwraps it while everyone looks on. Number two, and subsequent guests, have the option of taking away a gift already unwrapped, or selecting a new one. When a guest loses her gift, she selects another wrapped gift from the pile.

Hint: It adds to the fun if one prize is more valuable than the others so that it continually changes hands.

Human Tic Tac Toe
Team Game of Strategy

As in the paper-and-pencil game, Tic Tac Toe, the object is for one team to position X's and O's in a row, vertically, horizontally, or diagonally.

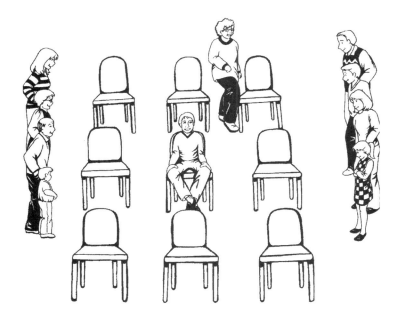

The difference is that people from opposing teams represent the X's and O's.

Any number more than ten can play, outdoors or inside. All that's needed are nine chairs (or places to sit). Any age can participate.

Begin by placing nine chairs in three rows of three chairs each to represent the squares of Tic Tac Toe.

Players, divided into equal teams, line up on opposite sides of the arrangement of chairs. Without any coaching from the team (except perhaps for small children), the first player in line selects a chair to sit in, followed by the first player from the opposing team. Teams alternate sending other players in sequence until one team wins or the "cat" gets it.

If any player already seated or in line give hints or influences the one whose turn it is, the other team wins that round.

Since players don't have X's and O's printed on their foreheads, part of the challenge is remembering which team the seated players belong to.

Relay Races
Win or Lose, It's Still Fun

Team games are entertaining to watch as well as to play. This is especially true of relay races that often become hilarious. Our parents used to enjoy watching from their lawn swing, perhaps holding one of the babies while the older children and adults participated in various types of relay races. Papa would tease the winners, and Mama would smile in sympathy at the losing teams.

The group divides into equal teams. At the signal, beginning with the first player, each member in turn does some action, often going to a specified mark and back. The first team to complete the action wins.

The skills used in the races are as endless as leaders' imaginations. Some old stand-bys continue to challenge players, but it is fun to tailor races to the occasion and put some significance to the actions that is meaningful to the group.

One example was the re-enactment of an old family caper when it rained. The older children stood on the then open porch when it began to rain and took turns running from the porch across the lawn to a nearby cedar tree and back to see who could stay dry the longest. We're not sure how popular this was with our mother, but the kids thought it was great fun.

Years later, we created a relay race based on that rainy day experience. Players lined up at the corner of the house (where the open porch once was) and ran to the same cedar tree and back, touching the next in line to take her turn. This game started many conversations and joking about the earlier incidents in the rain.

Another time we created a relay race using lunch buckets. We re-enacted the hectic time of getting us all off to school when we were kids. Players can imagine themselves in overalls, print dresses and ankle socks as they race to a line, fill a lunch bucket with an apple, sandwich, and cookie (or whatever the standard school lunch was in the family), run back to the next player who takes the bucket back, empties it, and returns for the next to repeat.

Some Traditional Relay Races

1. Run from one line to the other without dropping the rock balanced on the top of the wrist.

2. Carry a potato or an egg (depending on how daring or messy you want to be) in a spoon to the opposite line and back and then transfer it to the spoon of the next player. This version needs two spoons for each team. The first runner will give a spoon to the second person in line to be ready for the exchange.

3. Set a folded-up chair for each team at the opposite line. Each runner goes to the chair, unfolds it, sits down, gets up, refolds it, and returns to tag the next runner on the team.

Relays That Don't Require Running

1. Give each leader a hula hoop as teams line up side by side. Since a hula hoop relay does not require running, it is better suited for all ages. Players must pass the hoop over their body from head to toe before handing it to the next player in line. The team that first passes the hoop down the line of players and back to the leader is the winner.

2. Pass an orange, (or a softball-sized nerf ball, which we didn't have in our youth) that is held between the chin and shoulder, from person to person down the line and back again using only the chin and shoulder muscles. This is especially fun if the players vary in size, so that tall Shawn has to pass the orange to his short sister, Leah. If they drop it, they must start over.

3. Pass life savers from player to player using strong toothpicks held in the mouth.

4. Pass already prepared paper images of seasonal topics with a stirring straw (like those used to mix sugar in a coffee cup) held in the mouth. Jack-o-lanterns made from ordinary paper with the eye, nose, and mouth cut out to allow the straw to pass through an opening, paper cutouts of Easter baskets, flags, and Christmas trees are examples of seasonal objects. Anything works as long as there is at least one hole in the cutout.

5. Put on and take off a piece of clothing, such as an overcoat.

6. Sweep a small ball from one line to the other using an ordinary broom.

Relays For the Younger Set

There are many relays for little children. A few are crawl on hands and knees or hop on one foot to the line and back. Make a human wheelbarrow with one person holding the legs of another who walks on both hands. Race from one line to another and back again.

Upset the Fruit Basket
A Juicy Mixture

All players sit in a circle. Everyone chooses the name of a fruit. IT, who stands in the center, calls out the names of two fruits, such as apple and pear. As those two players exchange seats IT tries to steal one of their seats. If IT is successful, the player who lost his seat becomes IT. If not successful, IT calls out two other fruit names. At any time IT can say, "Upset the fruit basket." At that call, everyone must move to another seat. IT is sure to find a seat in the general confusion.

Forfeits
Heavy, Heavy Hangs Over Thy Poor Head

Forfeits is a favorite at many parties, either used as a game by itself or as the penalty for losing an earlier game. Adults enjoy it also. Players select a personal article to give

up. It may be a ball-point pen, a necklace, or even a shoe string.

One person sits in a chair blindfolded. The leader holds a personal article from another guest over the blindfolded one and begins this chant, "Heavy, heavy hangs over thy poor head. What must the owner do to redeem it?" The seated player, not knowing whose article it is, thinks up some action that the owner must perform in order to get back the item.

Some examples of actions might be: sing a song, run around the house, or (shockingly) kiss a boy. When the owner successfully does the action, that player gets the possession back and takes a turn in the chair as the blindfolded person who orders another guest to perform. The game continues until all players redeem their forfeits.

Hint: Eventually there is only one article and owner left. To avoid unfairness to this last person, the leader might intervene to make sure the action required is no harder or more embarrassing that the others.

What If?
Anything's Possible

Though not a real game in the true sense of the word, we have found that What If is fun and helps us understand one another on a deeper level.

Whenever the conversation dwindles down, someone may say, "What If you were forced to move someplace else in the world and you had all the money you needed to do it, where would you go?" Or, maybe, "What If you had to live for a whole week on only one kind of food, what would you chose?" Or "What If you could be anyone else in the world, who would it be?" Each person takes a turn answering. Then someone else can come up with another, "What If?"

This activity needs no planning or arranging; it's just a way to start interesting conversations. Usually more questions follow, such as, "Why did you choose that place?" or, "Do you think you would still like that food at the end of the week?"

3

Outside Games
Active Games

Outside Games

"Let's all go outside and play something," Judy might say as the conversation lagged at a family gathering. Everyone follows as Harold reminiscences that he held the title at Pleasant Ridge one-room country school as the last to get hit in Dodge Ball. Kathryn remembers being a running partner with a neighbor boy in Flying Dutchman. She couldn't run as fast as he did, so he literally drug her along with him.

Some of the younger generations look puzzled as we talk about these active outside games of our childhood. "We can't play games like that at school," they lament. "The teachers are afraid we will get hurt."

To be sure that our children get a chance to enjoy these time-honored active games, we include them in our family gatherings. A few of the games do get rough, but so do football and hockey. The over-sixty set has fun teaching the games and watching the youngsters play. The children love the games and learn new skills as they run, out-maneuver each other with strategy, and just plain have fun.

Less structured than competitive sports, these games can also enhance a youth's abilities. Learning to avoid a ball or to throw one at a target as in Dodge Ball teaches agility, accuracy, and strategy as well as the drills on a football field. The beauty of these games is that since they are not restricted to practice time, scheduled games and tournaments, all can play together on their own level of ability at any time a group wants something fun to do.

Most of these games are for warm weather, but a family favorite that was also played at many one-room schools needs a clean, new snowfall. Children trampled out a Fox and Geese course as soon as the snow stopped falling and spent hours running the circled paths until their lungs felt like bursting from the cold air. We preferred this game to snowball fights, but we admit we had our share of those also — usually from behind a well-built snow fort.

In our family, there is no game that can compare to Go Sheepie Beat It. At our last reunion, team members ranged in age from eighty-five-year-old Gertrude to three-year-old Shelbie. Each with some restrictions, Gertrude and Shelbie depend on other team members to compensate for those who can't run fast or don't understand the codes. A real sense of solidarity develops when ten people, crouched beside a prickly hedge, listen intently for coded directions from their leader. This game was a favorite of brothers Ralph and Vernon and remains a favorite among their children, nieces, and nephews.

Anyone who discusses the game Ante-Over has a different spelling. We have chosen Ante as our preference since using Anti sounds as if we are against something, and Anty (Auntie) appears to be speaking of a bug or a relative. Whatever the derivation of the word, we all agree that it is great to play, as it involves throwing, running, strategy, and team work. However, since the teams keep changing as players are captured, it doesn't demand intense team loyalty.

Light-hearted competition makes each of these games fun to play, interesting to watch, and good for muscle and skill development. The most important element is be included in a good time. Remember, we started out by saying, "Let's all go outside and play."

Go Sheepie Beat It
And Other Hiding Games

Participating in the game Go Sheepie Beat It is a coming-of-age ritual in the Gray clan. This game is our all-time favorite outdoor game. Even today relatives at a family gathering are greatly disappointed if we don't play it at least once. Miriam remembered Papa leading it at the community church when she was a little girl almost ninety years ago. But our special place to play it is our spacious lawn at The Wayside.

The game is commonly known as Run Sheep Run, but somewhere lost in family lore, one of our team captains, probably Ralph or Vernon, called out "Go Sheepie Beat It." That name stuck.

Like ordinary Hide and Seek, the first to touch the base wins. But unlike the simpler game, in Go Sheepie Beat It, players hide as a team and follow a strategy they work out with coded messages they all plan out together with their captain.

This hiding game needs two teams with a minimum of three players of any age and running ability, and a large outdoor area, which includes buildings, trees, walls, shrubs, ditches, or other places to hide a number of people. There are no boundaries or rules about where teams can hide. It is more fun to play at night.

Go Sheepie Beat It
Usually Called Run Sheep Run

To begin, the players agree on a centrally located base. After the big elm tree died, we use the sundial mounted on a marble pedestal in our open front lawn. Next, the players divide into two equal teams. Members of Vernon's team go into the house to "hide their eyes" while outside, Miriam's team hides.

Miriam's team must find a place big enough for all, as members must always stay together. They then make their plans. They agree on signals. "Sycamore" and names of trees may mean lie low, "Mississippi" and state names may mean move to the right around the house, and "Studebaker" and names of cars may mean get ready to run. When her team members have agreed on their strategy, she returns to the house alone. She accompanies Vernon's team, who must stay together in a group without straggling out. Miriam makes sure everyone stays together.

Those on Miriam's team may hide a long way from the base, and then obeying her shouted instructions, gradually move to closer, predetermined hiding places until she decides they are close enough to beat Vernon's team to the base. No one can run to the base until Miriam gives the signal everyone knows, "Go Sheepie Beat It."

As Vernon's team searches the area, Miriam calls out the coded instructions to her team. Often she shouts out meaningless words to confuse Vernon's team and to let her team know where the other team is by hearing her voice. At times she might show panic to fool Vernon into thinking his team is very near to the hidden ones. When Vernon's team finds them, or when Miriam believes her hidden team can reach the base first, she shouts, "Go Sheepie Beat It." At that call, and not before, all players run as fast as they can to the base. The first runner to touch it wins the game for that team. Vernon's team then takes a turn at hiding.

Hint: Even small children and not-so-active adults can play since not everyone has to run. The trick is to have at least one fast runner on each team. It is equally necessary to have a captain with a loud voice that will carry over the playing area. Being a physical education teacher, Miriam was a perfect choice. The captain must be imaginative and team members quick to respond.

It is a good idea for the hunting team to search first close to the base. One time Ralph hid his team in the moonlit shadows in the grass right by the base. The minute the other team straggled out of the living room door and stood by the stoop unsure which way to begin looking, Ralph yelled out, "Go Sheepie Beat It!" Of course, his team won easily. Ever since that long ago time, the searching team runs madly to the base the minute they get outside. The searchers also make sure the team is not lurking around the corner of the house waiting for the searching team to go the wrong way, thus opening the path to the base. Satisfied that the hidden team is not near the base, the team begins the search circling farther out.

Years ago we used to dodge under and through the barbed wire fence around our lawn, but for the safety of our children and grandchildren, we have removed the unneeded fence.

Miriam, Vernon, and Ralph are not with us anymore, but Vernon's daughters now initiate the game while Ralph's grandchildren have become the fast runners.

Hide and Seek
Tim, Seek My Base

At first we weren't going to include this universal favorite in our collection. Then we realized some people might not know all the rules. We agreed to include it.

Any number of people of any age can play Hide and Seek anywhere. The only things needed are hiding places and a base, which is often a tree or a marked space in the dirt. IT hides her eyes and counts slowly to a hundred while all others find a hiding place. Then IT hollers, "Here I come ready or not," and begins searching. The first one she catches and beats to the base will be IT in the next game.

When IT spots someone, she calls out, "Tim, seek my base." Tim races IT to the base. If IT beats him there he is the next IT. If he beats, then he is in free (won't have to be IT next game.)

When IT is tired of looking, supper is ready, or IT has either already caught someone or gives up the hunt, she can call out, "All-ie, All-ie outs in free." The other players come in without being caught.

Anytime during the game, hidden players can run to the base. If they tag it before IT does, they are in free.

Mother May I?
Mama Knows Best

This slow moving "race" takes place between two lines in a lawn or a building. Players line up on the beginning line. The object is to reach the opposite line and return first to the starting line. However, players move one at a time, in turn, following "Mother's" orders.

Mother (the designated leader for this round) says to the first in line, "Meg, you may take two giant steps." (Or baby steps, or scissors steps, or backward steps.) Meg must respond, "Mother, may I?" before moving forward. Mother answers, "Yes, you may."

If Meg moves without asking permission, she cannot advance on that turn. Mother says, "No, you may not." As in real life, Mother is in complete charge and can arbitrarily order the number of steps for each player.

Baby steps mean putting one foot directly in front of the other, heel to toe. Scissors steps mean swinging one leg across in front of the other in a scissor action while moving forward. Giant steps are as long as your legs will let you step without jumping. Backward steps mean turning around and taking steps any length you can manage while keeping your balance. An imaginative player can cover more ground by taking very large giant steps when Mother orders them.

Mother gives each player in turn her orders. If eager players begin their turn without asking Mother's permission, they lose their chance to advance. When they have success- fully reached the opposite line and returned to base, they go hide. The game then turns into regular Hide and Seek.

Variation: Sometimes players can sneak for- ward if Mother doesn't see them, like in Red Light, Green Light. If she catches them, they return to the starting line.

Another variation is to omit the hiding part.

Hint: Each player should have a turn at being Mother to avoid hard feelings if one Mother shows favoritism in assigning the steps.

Red Light, Green Light
Obey the Signals, or Maybe Not

As leader, David stands in front of the base line while the players facing him stand on a line about a hundred feet away. He can either turn his back or cover his eyes while he calls out, "Green light." Players then hurry toward the base line. When David turns around or uncovers his eyes to call out, "Red light," all players must stop in their tracks, even if one foot is in the air. If they move on "Red light" and David catches them, they must return to the starting line. David continues alternating the calls as players work their way to the base line. When players reach the base line they go hide as in Hide and Seek. The first one to reach the base line is the winner and becomes the new leader.

Part of the fun is trying to fool the leader by sneaking forward during "Red light." Leaders soon learn to watch people like Ruth closely, for she distracts them while inching closer to the base line without them catching her in the act.

Variation: Sometimes the hiding part is omitted.

Motion
Hide and Seek That May Never End

Motion adds an additional twist to Hide and Seek that keeps the game going longer and is more fun for everyone (except perhaps the one who is IT).

Begin Motion like ordinary Hide and Seek. Ann, who is IT, hides her eyes and counts to a hundred while all others hide. There is a base or pen around where Ann hides her eyes. As she locates a player, instead of the traditional race to the base, she tells the player to go straight to the pen. However, as the player goes, he calls out, "Motion, Motion." If those who are hiding wave to him without Ann seeing them (and thus being caught themselves), he has the freedom to run hide again. However, he will not try to run off until Ann isn't looking, for if she sees him and calls him back, he must wait for another motion.

Having to keep an eye on those caught limits Ann's activity, who must now watch those in the pen while searching for those hidden. If she doesn't see players escaping, they can hide again.

Players can escape only if the motion comes from someone hidden. A clever player in the pen will continue calling out for a motion even after receiving one, so Ann won't realize he is ready to escape again.

The game is over when Ann finds everyone and keeps them all in the pen together. The first one caught becomes IT for the next game.

Hint: The pen needs to be in an open area away from any obvious hiding place to give IT a better chance of seeing the escaping players.

Kick the Can
Another Longer Variation of Hide and Seek

Our older siblings brought home this favorite from our one-room school. In addition to at least six or seven players, it needs only an old tin can, or other similar object, placed in a square marked in the ground at the base.

Like Motion, the game begins with Hide and Seek and can go on for a long time as players have the option of hiding over and over again.

Unless IT is very experienced and can keep an eye on the base while finding the others, that player has difficulty catching everyone. The game ends when IT catches everyone and keeps them all together in the square at the base.

All players hide while IT counts to one hundred. When IT finds them, they must stay in the square, but if any of the players who aren't caught can sneak up to the can and kick it without IT seeing them before they kick the can, all caught players may run hide again.

After kicking the can, the player also hides again, but if IT spots him before he kicks it, he is caught. IT returns the can to its position and starts over. Since the players have to hide in the time it takes IT to return the can to its position, they kick the can as far as they are able.

Sardines
One Hides and the Others Seek

As a small child, Frances remembers first playing Sardines at night when visiting her Ohio cousins. Jane hid behind a telephone pole. In the dim light, the other players couldn't see the hiders as they lined up in the shadow of the pole.

Sardines reverses the usual pattern of Hide and Seek games. In this game all but one person hide their eyes while the one player, Jane, looks for a hiding place that will hold several people. After the required count of a hundred, the seekers individually search for Jane. When one by one they find her, they quietly join her in her hiding place, which usually becomes somewhat cramped, thus the name Sardines. The game ends when all seekers have joined the group.

The reward for being the first one to discover the hidden one is the chance to hide in the next game.

Hint: If other seekers are nearby when a player finds the hiding place, that player should amble on by without giving it away and slip into the spot unnoticed when others leave the area.

Ante-Over
And Other Throwing or Running Games

Children like nothing better than running, unless it is throwing. The following eleven games use one or the other and sometimes both skills. Even less active adults can play, or tiring out, they can sit by and watch the fun. A few of the games need some special attributes such as a small building in Ante-Over, newly-fallen snow in Fox and Geese, or eggs in Egg Toss, but most of the games require only eager players and space to play.

Ante-Over
A Popular Game at One-Room Schools

Ante-Over needs two teams of any age, a soft rubber ball, and a low building with space to run around all sides. This game was a favorite to play at the small, one-room schools. At The Wayside, the smoke house is the perfect building.

The team wins that "captures" all of the players of the opposite team by hitting them with the ball.

To begin, members of each team line up on opposite sides of the building where they cannot see one another. Someone from the team yells, "Ante-Over," and throws the ball over the building. If no one on the opposite side catches the ball before it hits the ground, someone retrieves it, yells, "Ante-Over," and throws it back.

If a player on the second team does catch the ball, the team as a unit runs around the building. The player who catches the ball tries to capture a player by throwing the ball and hitting a player from the other side with it.

There is suspense since players can't see what's happening on the other side of the building. They don't know if anyone caught the ball. Should they wait for the ball to be returned over the building or should they be ready to run? And which side of the building will their opponents come if they did catch the ball? When the team does appear, who is the one to avoid? All members of the team hold their hands behind them as if hiding the ball.

When team two comes into view, and not before, team one can run around the building. The player with the ball throws it at a fleeing player. If successful, that player then is "captured" and must join the other team. Players are safe when they reach the halfway mark around the building.

In running around the building, the teams have changed sides of the building. Team two retrieves the ball and from their new side of the building they yell out the warning, "Ante-Over." The game continues as they throw the ball over.

Keep Away
When Being Selfish Is Okay

Two teams of somewhat equal numbers play this ball game. One team forms a circle around the second team and throws a large, soft ball, such as a volleyball, over the heads of the enclosed team to other members of their own team in the circle. Those inside the circle jump up and try to capture the ball before it reaches the other team.

If someone intercepts the ball, then the thrower must join the opposite team. The action continues until one team captures everyone.

Variation: A less structured version eliminates the circle but lets the play take place anywhere in a given area of a yard or court. Team members throw the ball to another team member who can run in any direction to catch the ball and avoid the opponents.

Hint: Take care to divide the teams so that there are people of various sizes on each team.

Dodge Ball
Don't Let the Ball Touch You

Dodge ball is a team game that also involves throwing and running. One team forms a circle around the second team who can scatter themselves however they choose within the circle. Someone in the outside circle throws a large soft ball, trying to hit a player in the middle. If the thrower is successful, that player must join the other team. The winner is the last one left in the circle, the one who dodged the ball the longest.

Hint: The ball must be soft enough so that it won't hurt the players when it hits them.

Flying Dutchmen
Couples Running in Circles

We have never figured out why this game calls the runners Dutchmen, but we hope it is not intended as a slur of any kind. This very active game begins with all players but two in a large circle, holding hands. The two not in the circle must also hold hands as they walk, skip, or run around the outside of the circle until the runner nearest the circle taps a pair of joined hands as a signal to race. The tagged pair immediately starts running in the opposite direction from the couple who tagged them. Both couples, still holding hands, race back to the opening in the circle. The pair who reach it first join the circle, while the other couple become IT. The unsuccessful couple must continue around the circle choosing yet another pair of clasped hands to start another race.

Sometimes there is a difference in ages, and the pairs are unevenly matched in running ability. That doesn't matter. The faster runner must stay with the partner, not letting go of the hands while running around the circle.

This game is more fun if there are enough players to make a large circle. It was a favorite at the community ice cream suppers held in the church yard in Ellis near our farm. Everyone from first graders to young adults joined hands and took part.

Hint: To add suspense to the game, some runners outside the circle pretend they are going to touch a certain pair of hands and then pass on to surprise another pair.

Red Rover
Send Chip Right Over

Players form two equal lines, facing each other. They clasp hands tightly. Taking turns, they call out in unison,
"Red Rover, Red Rover,
Send Chip right over."
Chip runs to the opposite team and tries to break through the clasped hands. If he succeeds in breaking their hold, he chooses a player to take back to his team. If he is unsuccessful, he must join the team.
The team wins that gets all the members of the other team.

Hint: Small children should not play with older ones as they might get hurt. To avoid bruised hands, players often simply let the bigger players through.

Tag
You're IT, Evan

Like Hide and Seek, this is a universal favorite. Almost any place is fair game. Elizabeth comes up to her little cousin, Evan, in a large fellowship hall, tags him, and says, "You're IT." Then she

Family, Fun and Games: A Hundred Year Tradition

runs away from him as fast as she can. That's all it takes to start this running game. Evan chases her and the other children who are playing.

Two common types of tag are tree tag and squat tag. As the names suggest, the runner can touch a tree to be safe from IT, or simply squat down to be safe.

Three Deep
Two's Company, Three's a Crowd

In our family there is an argument over whether this game is called Three Deep or Two Deep. Carolyn is sure that it is Two Deep, but Ellen and Lester insist on Three Deep. You can see by the heading above who won!

Players choose partners and stand one in back of the other facing the same direction. The pairs arrange themselves roughly in a circle. Two people begin running with one chasing the other. If IT tags the runner, the positions reverse and the former runner becomes IT. However, a player can avoid being tagged by stopping in front of another pair. The third person in that little column then immediately becomes the one chased. As runners stop in front of other pairs, the partnerships continue to change as the ones behind get chased and stop in front of another pair. There are no winners or losers, just the fun of running, chasing, and finding a temporary resting spot in front of a pair of friends.

Cat and Mouse
Help the Poor Mouse

Players form a circle with hands clasped. One player is the cat and another the mouse. The cat tries to catch the mouse who runs around the circle, dodging under the clasped hands to escape. Players try to prevent the cat from catching the mouse by raising their hands to let the mouse through and lowering them to block the cat. When caught, the mouse joins the circle, displacing the one selected to be the new cat. The former cat becomes the next mouse.

Ice Cream and Lemonade
Play This Game If You're Not Afraid

This game contains elements of charades and tag. Any number can play as players divide into two teams that stand facing each other, each behind their own team line.

One team decides upon an action they will act out for the other team, such as riding a horse or washing dishes. They approach their opponents with this dialogue.

"Here we come."

The other team asks, "Where're you from?"

The answer is, "New York."

"What's your trade?"

"Ice Cream and Lemonade."

Then the opponents say, "Show us something if you're not afraid."

At this point the first team, in unison, without talking, acts out the action they decided upon earlier. The opponents try to guess, and when they do guess correctly, the first team runs back to their base line with the opponents chasing them. If any of the actors get tagged before reaching the base line, they must join the other team. Play alternates between sides and continues until all players get caught and are on the same side.

Hint: If the teams are evenly matched, the leader may need to call time or the game would get too tiresome.

Fox and Geese
A Game in the Snow

Even in the winter, it is fun to play games outside. Especially after being shut in the house during a snowstorm, family members can't wait to go outside to play in the newly-fallen snow. On a level, open area in the snow, they trample out the pattern of a maze.

The maze begins with a small circle, or the pen, which is large enough to hold several players. Surrounding that, spaced about eight feet apart, are two progressively larger circles. The paths joining the circles do not intersect. (See drawing.)

One player is the fox; the others are geese. The object is for the fox to chase and tag the geese one by one and put them in the pen. The fox and the geese must all stay in the paths. It's not fair to cut across. When the fox catches all the geese, the first one caught becomes the new fox.

Work-Up
Softball without Teams

Many times in the family or with neighbors, there aren't enough people to have two teams for softball. The solution is Work-Up, an adaption which uses the same rules as regular softball.

Work-Up needs at least seven to play. Players take their positions and rotate in this order: two or three batters, catcher, pitcher, first base, second base, third base, short stop, and fielders. If there are not enough players for all positions, they space themselves over the playing field to cover it.

A batter stays at bat until making an out. Then the player goes to right field. The catcher becomes the new batter, and all players move up one position.

Newcomers can join the game at any time by going to right field. If a player drops out, others simply move up or spread out over the field to fill the spot.

Without the restrictions and pressure of organized games, each player can participate in the fun so that everyone gains.

Egg Toss, Water Balloon Toss
Getting Messy Can Be Fun

Merle and Beth introduced this sport to a family gathering years ago. It is now a required activity at each reunion.

In an outdoor area partners line up across from each other in two lines about ten feet apart. Each pair has a raw egg (or a water-filled balloon). At the leader's command, players on one side of the line toss eggs to their partners standing in the opposite line. Anyone who fails to catch the egg must drop out of the action along with the partner.

After each toss, the leader asks each line to move back one step before the leader gives the order to throw again. This time players have reversed their throwing and catching roles. After each turn, pairs who drop the egg leave the game and those remaining increase the distance between them. The winners are the last ones without egg on their faces, or who haven't missed.

Balloons filled with water are less messy than raw eggs. Getting wet is fun on a hot day outside. Whether using eggs or balloons, there is a clean-up job to do afterward to remove broken shells or pieces of balloons.

4

Family, Friends, and Fun

Family, Friends, and Fun

Have you ever noticed that some families seem to have more company than others? Children often congregate in the lawns of one neighbor or friends drop in or look forward to invitations because they all like to be there. These spontaneous gatherings of friends are opportunities to start favorite games that we described earlier. Vernon's and Dorothy's lawn was such a place. Neighborhood children and parents congregated at their house, for there was always something fun to do.

However, creating an enjoyable atmosphere takes time and work. This section includes games and activities for gatherings with friends and extended family that involve prior planning.

The planning, which can be as much fun as the actual event, is essential for a successful occasion so that the host and hostess have as much fun as their guests.

Getting all guests involved quickly and seeing that no game gets tiresome or embarrassing to anyone is the key to success.

Many people today are not used to group participation games and may inwardly or outwardly groan when the host introduces a game.

As teenagers, Les and Chris were reluctant to get involved in People Bingo mixer until they paired up with some other cousins. Then they became quite competitive. Alicia and Elizabeth, who were younger, also paired up to get more information about this large group of relatives they were meeting.

After a successful mixer, start with a game that will appeal to all guests. Having a "stooge" in the group that echoes your enthusiasm helps.

The old saying, "Leave when you are still having fun," is very true.

Plan for lots of activities, but don't feel that you have to use them all. Stop the games (possibly by serving refreshments) while the players are still excited. The next party you have will be an even greater hit.

People Bingo
And Other Mixers

In almost any group gathered together for an event, there will be some people who know one another very well and some who know very few. In order to even the playing field, one or two mixers at the beginning of the event can benefit everyone. In addition to including newcomers immediately, a well-planned mixer works as an icebreaker that sets the mood for the rest of the occasion. Sharing laughter with a new friend or a new in-law forms a long-lasting bond. Mixers that encourage participants to actually get up from their seats and move around live up to the name mixer the best. Games such as People Bingo or Cobweb bring together the person sitting alone in a back seat into the close-knit group that clusters to talk.

Even in families, or maybe especially in families, an opportunity to let everyone get better acquainted right away is important. It can be overwhelming to be the new wife of a man with twenty-two cousins who are all hugging one another enthusiastically. It is equally intimidating (or maybe boring) to be a young teenager who doesn't remember very many people from the last get-together. A spirited mixer is the key.

People Bingo
Your Autograph, Please

People Bingo is a party mixer that works well with newcomers or with people who are acquainted to help them know even more about one another.

At a Gray family reunion, ten-year-old Jonathan was eagerly running around trying to fill in all the names on the People Bingo card but hadn't found anyone who had talked to a First Lady. Then he spotted ninety-year-old Harold. "Uncle Harold, did you find someone who has ever talked to a First Lady?"

Harold laughed, "I sure did. It was me, and I talked to Lady Bird Johnson when we planted a tree together on Arbor Day in Washington, D.C."

Jonathan was so interested in this story that he delayed his game to hear the whole story. As Jonathan left to continue his search for other signatures, he turned back to ask, "Why did they call her Lady Bird?"

This Texas boy and his great uncle from Washington, D.C. formed a bond. Harold was not just one of the older relatives at this gathering now but somebody who could tell about a lot of interesting historical facts.

People Bingo is effective with groups of any

size in any setting where there is space for people to move around freely.

The leader prepares and hands out to each player identical cards marked off with five squares in each of five rows, just like regular Bingo cards. Instead of having letters and numbers in the

PEOPLE BINGO

Get the signature of someone who can answer the following statements. A person can sign your card only once.

Went to a one room school	Has flown over an ocean	Is wearing red shoes	Kissed some one today	Can sing "The Bear Went Over the Mountain"
Plays a musical instrument	Has a cat	Skates with roller blades	Has marched in a band	Prefers baths to showers
Has ever walked on stilts	Is president of some group	Your name	Has cut down a tree	Enjoys playing chess
Has sewn a dress or shirt	Has seen GONE WITH THE WIND more than once	Has talked to a First Lady	Sings in a choir	Has gone to summer camp
Likes to eat licorice	Dislikes snakes	Dreams in color	Can ride a bicycle	Has an auto- graph of a celebrity

blocks, People Bingo has personal questions. The object is to be the first to "Bingo" by getting different signatures in every block in a straight line across, down, or on a diagonal. We find it more fun to play "Blackout Bingo" where the winner must have all squares filled.

At the start signal, players move around to get the signature of someone who can answer yes to the information within the block. Players can sign only one block on any given card. The leader can impose a time limit if no one calls out "Bingo" by filling out the required blocks.

After someone wins, we find it fun to discuss the card and learn more about one another. Which person was the most difficult to find? Who were the folks who attended a one-room school?

Obviously the game is tailored to the group that is playing it. In a family setting, the questions will relate to members of the family. If it is a club or church group, then the questions will have a theme appropriate to that group. Though the sample shown is made for a Gray family reunion with questions that each generation could answer, most of the questions are appropriate for any group.

Hint: It would be helpful to use cards stiff enough to give backing for the writer if the group is outdoors or not near tables. Also the leader should have extra pencils ready.

After the game was over and Jonathan was basking in the glory of being one of the first to get "Blackout," Harold finished their conversation. "Mrs. Johnson was called Lady Bird because a nurse gave her that nickname when she was a baby. I'm called 'Happy' because some college friends gave me that nickname. If you keep on playing games so quickly, you may be called 'Speedy'!"

Cobweb
Don't Get Tangled in the Web

When Ellen's guests arrived, she told them that they had to sit out in the lawn. They couldn't go into her living room because she hadn't had time

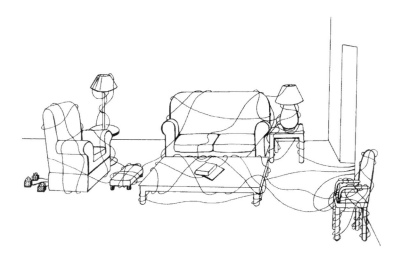

to clean out all the cobwebs. The guests exchanged glances. Familiar with her gatherings, they knew this was the beginning of a game.

When everyone was there, she asked them, "Will you each help me sweep out the cobwebs so we can go inside out of this heat?" Then she gave each one the end of a string that was tied to a stick. The string led them into the living room where it was interlaced with other strings in a web spread all over the room. Whether it is children or adults, once guests clear out the cobweb in the room, they are in a party mood.

Cobweb works with any age. Depending on the size of the room, up to fifteen or twenty people can play. This game needs lots of light string, like kite string, a small prize for each person, and some prior preparation.

Before the guests arrive, prepare the cobweb. One strand at a time, unwind a string for each guest all around the room. At the door, tie the start of the strand to a chair leg or a stick weighted down so it will stay in place. Go under chair legs, over and around furniture, back and forth across the room hooking around anything you have. When you come to the end of the strand, tie some favor, joke, or other prize and hide it under a cushion or some place that isn't obvious. When you have finished stringing out all the different strands of string, you truly have a cobweb.

Give all players sticks to wind up their strand and turn them loose. The only rule is that they can't break the string. This isn't a race, as all get something, just by untangling their own strings. Guests will have to step over, crawl under, and otherwise maneuver through the cobweb to follow their own strand to the end.

Variation: Giving guests opposite ends of the same string is one way to form pairs. When they meet in the middle, they find their partner.

Hint: If you have more than one door to the room, it relieves congestion to split the starting point.

Be careful to put the strings around non-breakable objects. Lamps, knick-knacks, and pictures could be damaged as players put pressure on the strings.

Using a different color of string for each player helps keep track of individual strands in case they do break accidentally. It looks pretty even though not many spiders spin colored webs!

Toilet Paper
Take What You Need

This mixer begins with the leader passing a large roll of toilet paper around the room. The only instruction is, "Take what you need." After everyone pulls off a share of the paper, the leader explains the game. Many people take a lot while others may pull off only a small piece.

In turn all players stand and tell something about themselves. Bill might say he is from Connecticut, that he has one son, that he commutes to New York City each day — whatever pieces of information he wants to tell the group. For each fact he gives about himself, he tears off a piece of paper. When he is out of paper, he must sit down and stop talking.

Sometimes it is hard to get people to say anything, and other times it is hard to get them to stop. This game predetermines how long each person will speak.

Lies and Truth
I'm Not Sure I Believe That!

Lies or Truth is a good get-acquainted game for a large group. The leader asks the guests to form groups of no more than four or five. The

159

mixer begins. Each person tells the others four things about themselves. Three of these things must be true facts. The fourth will be a lie. The lie should be mixed in with the true facts. The group then guesses which bit of information is the lie.

To make it more fun, the guests make their true facts rather unusual, with the lie something as deceiving as the date of one's birth, or the number of grandchildren.

At a recent Elderhostel, Carolyn heard one of the guests say she had been sky diving, sang on a radio show, had three sons, and dyed her hair blue when she was in college. The lie was that she had three sons. Conversation follows these true experiences. Most remember these unusual things about their new friend.

Hint: There needs to be a time limit for this mixer or it can generate so much conversation that the rest of the evening's activities may get short-changed. The leader needs to monitor the groups to be sure that each person has a turn to tell four facts.

A Noncents Party
Working with a Theme

For this theme party that Carolyn gave, each invitation had a shiny new penny pasted onto the front of the card. Inside the card it read, "You are invited to a NONCENTS PARTY at _____, on _____. You'll need your cents to get in. Please bring this invitation with you."

As the guests arrived, Carolyn gave each an end of a piece of string and told them to wrap it around their invitation. They followed the string around the corner into the living room where they saw a cobweb of strings (see p.156). When they reached the end of the string after working through the tangles of other guests' strings, they found another penny on a note that said, "Now you have your two cents worth."

After everyone completed the Cobweb, the guests entered into another room with hidden pennies. Each guest was supplied with a small container, a change purse, a small paper bag, a cloth bag with a drawstring tie, or simply an envelope. A version of an Easter egg hunt with each person searching for pennies followed.

Next came a paper and pencil game that was answered with words containing the letters C E N T. (see p. 171) You guessed it, the winner won five more pennies.

The guests then had a Treasure Hunt (see p. 178) with the clues leading to a roll of fifty pennies. The treasure hunt is effective either with individuals or small teams. If it is done in teams, leave a roll of pennies for each member of the winning team.

Refreshments for the party were served at a table with pennies on the place cards. For less formal arrangements, you could glue pennies on napkins. At our party, the refreshments imitating the look of new pennies were orange sherbet, small round golden-colored cookies, and an orange drink. Nut cups held Cheese-Its and Cheese Curls.

Glued on the bottom of one guest's dessert plate was a penny. She won the door prize (two rolls of pennies). At the end of the evening, the one with the most money received the party prize, a small calculator to help in adding up the money. No one went home empty-handed, for each guest kept any pennies collected or won.

Actually, the party doesn't end up costing any more than buying prizes for different games. And everyone has a little money to take home.

Ellen created a similar party using buttons instead of pennies. Since Carolyn doesn't sew and have enough buttons, she prefers the penny theme. What do you think about it? A penny for your thoughts.

Crazy Intelligence Test
And Other Paper and Pencil Games

Paper and pencil games are standards for many club meetings. They provide self-test amusement and work well also for family gatherings. The common type of quiz that you find in many magazines, newspapers, and game books are fun and challenging. However, we have limited this type of game to a few family-oriented quizzes and one that was used at a theme party. Individual families can develop quizzes with names of actual relatives, places where the family lived, occupations, and hobbies of people in the family. Word searches such as the one designed by Miriam for a Christmas club meeting are also successful, especially if you are looking for your own name in the puzzle. These games need only enough pencils and paper for all guests.

Crazy Intelligence Test
When the Wrong Answer Is Right

This game isn't how much you know, but whether you can give the wrong answer. It works well with any age old enough to write "yes" or "no." It can be a time killer, a quiet game between more active ones, or included in a series of serious pencil and paper games to give a bit of levity.

Players number to twenty down the left side of a piece of paper. The leader tells the group to write beside each numbered question a "Yes" or "No." But the answer must be the wrong one. For instance, to the question, "Does a house have a roof?" the answer is "No." The leader then reads the following questions (or any that may fit the group better) one after another quickly without giving much time to think. We are so programmed to give the right answer that players will be surprised how hard it is to give a wrong one.

1. Is it cold at the North Pole? No
2. Is the moon made of cheese? Yes
3. Are oranges black in South Dakota? Yes
4. Does water flow up hill in China? Yes
5. Does a car use gasoline in the radiator? Yes
6. Will paper burn upside down? No
7. Can a dog bark after it is dead? Yes
8. Are bananas good to eat in Siberia? No
9. Are lemons sweet in California? Yes
10. Is Honolulu near the Atlantic Ocean? Yes
11. Is gasoline inflammable? No
12. Are green apples good for indigestion? Yes
13. Is snow white on a coal pile? No

14. Is gold valuable when lost? No
15. Is a sweet potato a vegetable? No
16. Is baking soda poisonous? Yes
17. Is strychnine good for baby colic? Yes
18. Does kerosene taste good in milk? Yes
19. Are Caucasians red? Yes
20. Does January come in the summer? Yes

Variation: For family gatherings, the questions could all be about family members. People like it when their name is mentioned. For instance, questions getting in family names might be something like, "Gordon's and Janice's children, Matt, Dan, and Tim are all girls." Yes. Or, "The two Dans are twins." Yes.

Grade the papers. The winners are those who get all answers right (or is it wrong?) Either way, it's crazy.

Examination
A Transition Game to Dinner

Ellen adapted this game to a group of writers at a twenty-four hour retreat at her house. Creative people can gear the questions to fit any group. This game works best as a relief if part of the activities during the day have been serious.

Tell your guests in a serious tone that you are giving them an examination over what they've learned (or been doing). Ask them to number to fifteen down the left side of the paper. Read aloud the following instructions and ask the guests to write the proper letters under the proper numbers. Be sure all understand the question and give them enough time to follow instructions.

1. If you ever wrote an encyclopedia of auto mobile parts, write "yes" in spaces 6 and 11. If you did not, put an "R" in those spaces.

2. If X comes before H in the alphabet, write Z in spaces 2 and 8. If it comes after H, write I.

3. If a book is longer than an essay, write E in spaces 5 and 12. If not, put a W for What kind of writer are you, anyway?

4. If you like writing on a computer better than on a slate with chalk, indicate with an S in space 9. If not, better quit writ ing at once.

5. Closing one eye and without counting on your fingers, write the next to last letter of the alphabet in space 15.

6. If Shakespeare wrote "Twinkle, twinkle, little star, How I wonder what you are," put O in space 13. Otherwise write A.

7. If Walt Whitman was ten feet tall, write M in spaces 7 and 10. If not, write nothing there.

8. If Steven King writes for *Time* magazine, draw an elephant in spaces 3 and 4. Otherwise write N.

9. If you think this is foolish, write the fourth letter of the alphabet in spaces 1 and 14. Read the result and follow me.

The guests who successfully pass the examination will find that their letters when read down the page spell "Dinner is ready."

Variation: Ellen uses a variation of this game with her students when classes fall on April Fool's Day. She tells them they will have a pop quiz. Of course, there is the usual moaning and groaning. Then she asks questions about what they have been studying, but ones so easy that no one can miss them. Each question becomes more ridiculous. Quick students will realize that the letters spell, "April Fool" before she has them fill in the last letters.

Christmas Puzzle
Search for the Words

Miriam made the following word search puzzle for a December 1993 meeting of the Ellis Domestic Science Club, which was organized by our mother in 1915. She asked members to find the twenty-three words relating to Christmas in the grid below by reading up, down, forward, backward, or diagonally. Leftover letters name a biblical village in the Christmas story.

```
S  U  A  L  C  A  T  N  A  S
A  L  O  S  S  T  E  E  L  S
M  O  O  Y  T  B  A  E  T  L
T  T  O  R  R  F  H  N  L  E
S  T  A  R  A  O  I  N  N  I
I  S  N  O  W  C  F  G  C  G
R  I  D  E  K  E  H  Y  R  H
H  A  P  P  Y  C  Y  R  A  M
C  J  E  R  U  S  A  L  E  M
E  Y  O  J  O  S  E  P  H  M
```

CAROLS, JERUSALEM, SLEET, CHRIST-MAS, JOSEPH, SLEIGH, FOR YOU, JOY, SNOW, GIFTS, LOOT, STAR, HAPPY, MARY, ST. NICK, HEAR, PACK, TEA, ICY, RIDE, TOYS, INN, SANTA CLAUS

What Is It?
See If You Can Guess

We customized this puzzle to fit our family. By changing the answer and the names, you can quickly come up with a puzzle to fit your group.

Deborah has it before.
Ed has it behind.
The Grays never had it.
All ladies have it once.
Gentlemen cannot have it.
Dudley has it twice.
David has it before and behind.

No matter how hard they tried, Barbara, Jerry, Kristi, and Sue couldn't get it.
But Sandy, Gordy, Randy, and the rest of the kids want it just before the end.
What is it?

Answer: The letter "D."

Scrambled Relatives
Who Can Keep Them Straight?

Our family keeps getting all mixed up about our relations. Can you help us straighten this out? Unscramble each jumbled word or phrase to identify a family member.

1. RTAFHE
2. NCOSIU
3. THRADGMRENO
4. ROTHERB
5. TRESSI
6. TUNA
7. CENIE
8. WHENPE
9. CELUN
10. TOMRHE
11. SSNIKIG NICOUS
12. NEDCOS SNOCUI
13. RADTHUGE
14. TELDES SNO
15. YABB TREISS

Answers: 1. Father; 2. Cousin; 3. Grandmother; 4. Brother; 5. Sister; 6. Aunt; 7. Niece; 8. Nephew; 9. Uncle; 10. Mother; 11. Kissing cousin; 12. Second cousin; 13. Daughter; 14. Eldest son; 15. Baby sister.

A Centsible Game
It Makes Sense

To get your money's worth from this game you find a word that fits each of these definitions. But your word must have C-E-N-T in that order within the word. Here goes:

1. A small worm   _ _ _ _ _ _ _ _

2. Going Up   _ _ _ _ _ _ _ _

3. A hundred years   _ _ _ _ _ _ _ _

4. Coming down   _ _ _ _ _ _ _ _

5. Not long ago   _ _ _ _ _ _ _ _

6. Tone of voice   _ _ _ _ _ _ _ _

7. Wonderful   _ _ _ _ _ _ _ _

8. Reserved in speech   _ _ _ _ _ _ _ _

9. Odor   _ _ _ _ _ _ _ _

10. Every hundred years   _ _ _ _ _ _ _ _

11. Old-time telephone operator _ _ _ _ _ _ _

12. Roman soldier _ _ _ _ _ _ _ _

13. Decorative table arrangement _ _ _ _ _ _

14. Middle _ _ _ _ _ _ _ _

15. Emphasize _ _ _ _ _ _ _ _

The answers are: Centipede, Ascent, Century, Descent, Recent, Accent, Magnificent, Reticent, Scent, Centennial, Central, Centurion, Centerpiece, Center, Accentuate.

Broom Football
And Other Team Competitions

Being a part of a team lets each person participate, and allows the skills and abilities of each one to complement the others on the team. When the teams consist of people of various ages and abilities, it is exciting to watch a sixty-year-old grandmother competing with an eight-year-old grandson as they sweep the puck under a chair in Broom Football. Her years of experience with a broom outweigh the child's quickness and energy.

You have to watch it though. Sometimes grandmothers let their grandchildren win on purpose!

Seeing a dignified uncle blowing a ping pong ball across a table can change a young child's perception of older people. Likewise, the older uncle can appreciate the warmth that comes when teammates congratulate him on being windy.

Being part of a team exemplifies what is best in families--that is, everyone working for the good of all. Good families and good games. They go together.

Broom Football
Sweeping Your Team to Victory

If you can find two brooms, a small object that can be moved with a broom (preferably soft and irregular like a sponge), and a flat surface, you are ready to play Broom Football. Oops, you also need two straight chairs to use as goals.

Divide the group into two teams that line up facing each other about eight feet apart. Set the chairs as goals at each end of the lines, half way between the players. Place the brooms on the chairs and the puck in the middle between the two chairs and the two lines of players. For each team, number off the players starting with one. Reverse the numbers on the opposite team. That means, number one on team A is at the opposite end of the line from number one on team B.

The leader, who does not participate, calls out a number. The player with that number runs to the right, picks up a broom, comes back to the puck, and tries to sweep it under his chair (the one to his right). At the same time, the player on the other team with that number does the same thing and tries to get the puck away from her opponent or keep the puck from going under his goal(chair). Players can use nothing but brooms. If the puck goes out of the playing field, the area between the two lines and

the two chairs, the leader blows a whistle or yells stop. The leader returns the puck to its center position as play resumes.

The leader keeps score and is careful to call every number so that each player gets a turn. The game continues until one team has scored ten points or until everyone has played.

Hint: It is more fun if the leader varies the order of calling the numbers. When there is only one number not yet called, everyone will expect to hear that number. The leader can surprise the group by calling another one instead. However, the game will not stop until all numbers have been called.

It is fairer if the two brooms are similar sized and in similar condition.

Ping-Pong Football
When It's Good to Be a Blowhard

Don't play this game if the flu bug is going around!

Divide players into two teams with captains. Teams kneel on opposite sides of a child's table or coffee table. The captain of each team is at either end of the table. Put a ping-pong ball in the middle of the table. All players try to blow the ball off the end of the table guarded by the opposing captain. The captain, of course, blows the ball back if possible with the help of teammates. If the ball goes off the sides of the table, place it back at the point where it went off.

Players get so tickled that they sometimes can't blow for laughing.

Although players can't use any part of their bodies, if the ball bounces off of a player on the sidelines and comes back onto the table, it does not disrupt the play.

Players must remain on their knees unless they are too short to see over the side of the table. Players who can't kneel comfortably can

sit on a low stool as long as their heads are at the same level as the other players.

Variation: Everyone must do the blowing through a straw.

Frisbee Golf
Teeing Off with Disks

This game needs some simple advance preparation. The leader fastens numbers from one to nine onto trees in a large grassy area. Each player on each team (no more than four members) has a frisbee that has some marking on it to identify it. In turn, players throw their frisbees toward tree number one. After all players have had a turn, they find their frisbees and throw again until the disc touches tree number one. They keep track of the number of throws as in regular golf. This continues with tree number two through nine, playing all nine "holes."

The team with the lowest number wins. The overall winner is the one who completed the course with the fewest throws.

Variation: Two people can play the game, or even one practicing for a better score.

Treasure Hunt
Follow the Clues

"The game I liked best was the one where you had clues on pieces of paper," said John. An only child who knew nothing about family games until he married into the Gray family, he hadn't joined in any games. That is, not until he became part of a team in Treasure Hunt. Then he was hooked on games.

People of any age can participate in this favorite game. The object is to be the first team to successfully follow all the clues on the trail to a hidden treasure. Since the game is always different, depending on the imagination of the leaders, the setting for the game, and how mobile the players are, the Gray family plays it over and over at gatherings. It can be played almost anywhere, indoors or out.

While most of the games in this book take very little preparation, this game requires much thought and preparation. Materials needed are different colored papers on which to write the clues and some treasure. It is helpful to have at least two people plan the routes, write out the clues, and place the clues for the teams to find.

First the leaders need to find ten to twelve locations suitable for hiding folded written clues where they won't be noticed, blown away, or otherwise damaged until the game begins. Next the leaders compose the clues (sometimes in verse form) for each location.

For players on foot, the big lawn and entrance way at The Wayside is an excellent place to have a treasure hunt. However, some treasure hunts expect the teams to use cars. In Washington, D.C., once Miriam had a treasure hunt that required players to drive all over the city. Or the search could be restricted to a building or house.

At our last big reunion Gertrude, her daughter, Sarah, and granddaughters, Hayley and Ellery, limited the hunt they prepared to the farmstead. Following are some examples of the hiding places and their clues that Hayley and Ellery wrote.

Seth Thomas Clock:

Look by Grandfather's clock, which still goes tick tock.

Smokehouse:
The smoke from the heat

Preserved their meat.
Corner post:
Many cousins have tested their fate
By climbing the old Wayside gate!
Work Bench:
You'll find a clue and a wrench
On this messy indoor bench.

Next they figured out a system to put the clues in the chosen hiding places so that each team will go to the same hiding places but not in the same order. To assure they pick up the correct clue, for each team, Hayley used a different color of paper and numbered each team's clues in order. If the red team finds a clue in a hiding place, but the number is not the correct one, that team hasn't correctly solved the last clue. The team must leave that clue until finding the right clue in the prescribed order.

When all players are ready, divide the group into equal teams, with different generations in each team.

The only rules are that the team members must find the clues in numerical order. They must not look at or bother the other teams' clues, and in order to keep the treasure, they must bring all clues to the leader.

The team does not have to stay together. If the clue reads, "Here you might find a letter, and you'll be one clue the better," meaning the next clue is in the mailbox a quarter of a mile up the driveway, only one person needs to run that distance. Or it is permissible for an ingenious Michael to load his team into his pickup and drive up there.

Hint: To make the game more satisfying and assure that all teams continue to the end, prepare several treasures. Instead of having just one treasure at the end, have treasures of different values for everyone at the end — either something the team can share, or individual items. The first team gets to choose the prize they want.

This game is sometimes played at Christmas, where people must follow clues to find their presents.

Scavenger Hunt
A Race to Get Everything on the List

Another game that requires advance preparation is Scavenger Hunt. The leader makes out lists of items for the players to find and bring back. He divides the group into teams of no more than five, gives each team identical lists, and tells them that the first team back with all items wins.

The list might include such things as an Indian head penny, or it could be something like Thelma's, Stephanie's, and Janice's signatures. In the past, some of our scavenger hunts used the car as players raced all over the area. Now we prefer for safety's sake to restrict the players to places they can go on foot.

The winning team should get a prize that all team members can share, such as a sack of candy.

Variation: Substitute information instead of items to bring back. People can learn about their family or area by questions such as, "What is Margie's maiden name?" "What is Grandpa Gray's middle name?" or, "Whose picture is in the middle of the framed picture in the hall?" Other questions could be simply, "How many steps are on the front sidewalk," or, "How many windows are on the east side of the house."

This game is easy to turn into an information hunt relating to some theme or subject of the gathering. Family information, if a family reunion, Bible facts if a church group, plant trivia if a garden club. You get the idea. It is limited only by your imagination.

Circle Scavenger Hunt

A simpler variation is Circle Scavenger Hunt. Two or three small teams use the same list of items to bring to the leader, but they must find all of the items from the people in the circle. This list could have such items as a black shoelace, a bobby pin, a quarter, or a blue sock. The goodwill of those not on the teams lets them be part of the fun while not having to run around. Of course, team members can pool their own assets for the items as well as those in the circle.

5

Reunions, Fun, and Games

Reunions, Fun, and Games

I can't believe that over eighty people from all over the country come every four years to your family farm," said one of Kathryn's friends from her retirement home in Connecticut. The friend shook her head in disbelief. "And stay for three days!"

Ellen's neighbor in Missouri said, "Our family lives within easy driving distance, and we do well to get half of them together for one meal. The kids don't want to come. All we do is eat and talk to those we already know. There's very little mingling or doing anything else. What do you do to make your reunions so successful?"

Carolyn and Ellen know what to do. For years they have chaired family reunions and other group gatherings. It takes three things, planning, preparing, and involving everyone.

Since we believe that family is most important,

we work at it, making plans, corresponding, and checking local facilities months in advance.

After our father's death, we remember our mother sitting in the lawn swing before her own death in 1969. She looked out over the yard where her children and grandchildren played and to the fields beyond. She wondered aloud what would become of the farm she loved and whether we would all keep in touch with one another. If she were alive today, in the lawn that looks very much as it did in her lifetime, she could see two of her great-great-granddaughters who live there playing with their stuffed animals. She'd know that ninety percent of her descendants come to the farm every four years.

"Yes, Mama, we've kept the farm. And second and third cousins know one another from the regular reunions."

This extended family togetherness doesn't just happen. It takes much planning and preparing so that everything goes smoothly. However, all the preparation is wasted unless all who come thoroughly enjoy themselves. That's where everyone participating comes in.

Since interests vary widely from babies to those in their nineties, the key is in variety. Have some activities geared for a certain age, such as wading pools for pre-schoolers, volleyball for older children, and memorabilia for grandparents. Then there must be activities for everyone to enjoy together, such as many of the games described in previous sections, family skits, and a series of activities throughout the gathering based on a theme. Don't forget that some people enjoy the visiting that bores many youngsters. Save time for that.

This section gives some samples of specific activities that have been successful in the Gray family reunions. Copy them, adapt them to your special group, or better yet, let them be a spring board for your own imagination to come up with a unique reunion for your group.

Siblings Gossip
Dear Brothers and Sisters...

When Carolyn left home, the original eight brothers and sisters began a round robin called Siblings Gossip. Many years later Ellen compiled the letters into book form to give to each sibling and their children. At one reunion Ann took excerpts from the book for a reading she presented in front of the entire group. The original siblings did not read the excerpts from their letters. She assigned them to one of their children.

Following are excerpts from one reading we did

based on those early letters. Every family has some written materials, letters, records, diaries, or memoirs that with some imagination can be prepared for special gatherings. Or ask people before the gathering to each write something to read.

MIRIAM - July 1944, Austin, Texas

Dear Siblings,
Here goes! Since I am the eldest in the family, it seems appropriate for me to begin a sort of round robin to circulate to all eight of us so we can keep closer touch with one another.

I'll begin with a college joke my students tell. Did you hear what the mayonnaise said to the icebox? Keep the door closed, I'm dressing.

KATHRYN - July 28, 1944, Terre Haute, Indiana

Now you are really going to have to dig in and work--reading my charming long hand. Too bad we have no typewriter. Anyone want to send me one?

RALPH - August 2, 1944, Green Meadows, Maryland

I'll confess that most of the delay of the robin was due to me. The reason was that it took me seven days to figure out all of Kathryn's hiero-glyphics. I'm writing this on a typewriter I borrowed from a neighbor. Don't you have neighbors, Kathryn? With typewriters?

VERNON - August 6, 1944, Cleveland, Ohio
I work at the Aircraft Engine Research Laboratory of the National Advisory Committee for Aeronautics. I'm a War Service employee for the duration of the war plus six months.

RALPH - September 3, 1944
Jean said if these letters keep coming around so often, she'll cancel her membership in the Literary Guild.

KATHRYN - February 1945
Katie Gray has started to kindergarten. Before she started she couldn't put on her leggings. At least not without an awful lot of fuss. After only three days at school, she came home one day to tell me about a girl that was five and a half years old who couldn't even put on her snow suit. Education is a wonderful thing!

HAROLD - February 20, 1944, Chicago, Illinois
Chicago has browned out 100%. The only out-

door lights left are street lamps, and alternate ones of the brightest of them are off. Same is true in Detroit, Columbus, Milwaukee, and Lansing, to give you an idea of Midwest patriotism and my travels lately.

MIRIAM - August 1, 1944

You've no doubt heard the Texan's prediction of how long the war will last. It will take a year to beat Hitler, another year to lick the Japs, and three years to get the damyankees out of Texas.

HAROLD - November 11, 1944

Gordon has gained a pound since birth and is quite handsome. Lida and I seem to be getting along about as well with three as we did with two in this diminutive firetrap. Gordon gets six feedings per day which cuts into our sleep as much as nights out with the boys did in better, I mean, earlier days.

KATHRYN - November 17, 1944

Dudley and I are planning a trip to Indianapolis the Saturday after Thanksgiving and we are driving, no less. We seem to have enough gas to go. [gas rationing] We haven't been more than five miles out of town in our car since we arrived here a year ago.

CAROLYN - March 21, 1945, Columbia, Missouri

Even little Columbia has browned out. As a result, on week-nights the lights on our avenue are turned off. It gives our house-mother a great deal of worry.

VERNON - April 29, 1945

To date this issue let me add that during this weekend: Russia captured Berlin and U.S. took Munich, the end and the beginning of Nazism; also Mussolini was shot and defiled, the Italian war ended; U.S. and Russian forces joined in Germany; and Himmler tried twice to surrender the country.

RALPH - May 11, 1946

I guess I am the first in the Robin to wish Carolyn a long and happy married life and to welcome Lester to the In-law Self-protective Association. Anyway, Carolyn, there hasn't been so much excitement in the family since Papa's horse ran out of oats on the way home from the pie supper in 1902. [The year he proposed to our mother.] Our pride in you is matched only by our astonishment that "little Carolyn" is old enough to marry.

GERTRUDE - June 7, 1945, Bethesda, Maryland

The Toths really got out of their rut this time. Alex sailed for London June 4th, our wedding anniversary. [A new job] He said that I'd had seven fat years, and now I should have seven lean years, because even if Sandy and I do go over there soon, he will be leaner.

ELLEN - May 24, 1946, Lebanon, Missouri

I have finally finished school after two degrees and am working at being a home demonstration

agent with the agricultural extension office. I come to you from Lebanon, Missouri. It is in the Ozarks. If you want beautiful scenery and interesting people, here is the place to come. I've really taken to the hills.

GERTRUDE - 1947

It was sure good to get back [from England] into a modern house again. Sandy had a pretty bad time for two weeks. He was so completely English, and he had forgotten so many things. Ice cubes he didn't know. The thing that fascinated him the most was the light in the refrigerator and he couldn't understand how we could have hot water without a fire in the stove.

ELLEN - October 1947

Lane and I have bought a small farm near the village of Morgan. It is forty acres of hill pasture. The house is not modern; it doesn't even have electricity, though we should be able to get that soon. But all in all it seems a pretty good setup.

CAROLYN - December 9, 1947

Speaking of modern conveniences, we had a nice visit with Ellen and Lane over Thanksgiving. They have the nicest outhouse. Really. It is so new it smells of good old oak lumber and is quite pleasant except for a decided draft.

Are We There Yet?
Family Skit

Combining family lore into an entertaining skit is fun for the writer, the actors, and the audience. The Gray family for many years "commuted" each summer from their farm in western Missouri to their winter residence in Washington, D.C. for the school year. These twice-yearly road trips with a family of eight children created many good and not-so-good memories of family togetherness.

At one of our reunions, Carolyn's family presented a skit about these trips. She set up two benches, one about three feet behind the other. In between the benches were two folding camp stools.

Son-in-law, Mark, narrated the skit explaining that all of the family members were entering the car from the driver's side because all the luggage was on the right running board behind a folding gate and covered with a tarp. Carolyn played the role of Mama, with her youngest, six-foot-tall daughter, Susan, playing a pre-school-aged Carolyn. The scene opened with Papa, played by nephew, David, calling for Kathryn and Gertrude (daughters-in-law Jenny and Joan) to hurry because we were leaving.

Kathryn complains about the lack of a trunk and doesn't see why we can't have a car with a trunk like the Mannings do. Everyone settles in with Papa, Harold (son Michael) and Kathryn in the front seat. Mama with Carolyn on her lap, Gertrude and Ralph in the back seat with Vernon and Ellen (son Mark and daughter Shirley) back to back on the stools in between.

The trip commences with Mama asking if anyone has checked the battery water (a common concern she had), Carolyn needing to go to the bathroom again, Ellen and Vernon fussing that the other was crowding, and Harold making a suggestion that we take a more scenic route to see the state capitol buildings. Gertrude tries to comfort Ellen in her competition for room with Vernon, and Ralph wants to start a game. As the action progresses, Mama suggests that we sing to pass the time. Everyone starts singing a different song at the top of their lungs, but Carolyn wants to stretch out and take a nap across the laps of Gertrude, Ralph, and Mama. They say that it is Harold's time to choose where they will eat the first meal, and Carolyn complains that when it gets her time to choose, it will be three days later.

All of these actions were typical of the car

trips. The oldest child, Miriam, usually conveniently had a summer camp job or other employment so she was not often on the trips. A highlight of the skit was when Papa became tired of the arguments between Vernon and Ellen and without looking away from the road swiped anyone within his reach in the back seat with his right arm. Vernon ducked, but Ellen got the brunt and started crying. Gertrude tried to comfort her again.

Writing typical reactions of each person into the skit gave those watching not only a glimpse of what the car trip was like, but also an insight into their relatives' characters.

This skit dramatized a recurring activity. Other skits could immortalize a one-time important action, such as when Papa took Mama on their first date, or when the other seven sibling found out that Mama was pregnant again for the eighth time. Every family has funny, dramatic, or historic moments that are easy to dramatize. Depending on the occasion, it's probably better not to make skits out of the sad times. These are better preserved in written form, in music, or poetry.

The important thing is to allow each generation to learn a little more about those who went before them.

Now for the Big Reunion
Examples and Ideas That Have Worked

When Gertrude asked her granddaughter what she liked best about the last reunion at The Wayside with eighty-two relatives attending for three days, Ellery answered, "Getting acquainted with all of my cousins."

Her answer made all the planning and preparing worthwhile, for that is what reunions are all about — togetherness. She and her sister Hayley conducted a very successful Treasure Hunt, amazing her great-aunts and other relatives with their leadership and organizational abilities, (not to mention coming up with rhymes at a moment's notice). But what impressed her was not the highly successful game, but being with Leah, Shawn, Jeff, Brad, Elizabeth, and Alicia.

Isn't that what reunions are for? Now these young people have memories that they can share

years hence when they prefer more sedentary visiting to the active games they played on their great-grandparents' lawn.

To help others put on a big reunion, we have summarized some of the procedures and activities that have worked for us since our first big reunion in 1953 at our parents Golden Wedding Anniversary.

After the planning, correspondence, and local arrangements are complete, the guests arrive for their first impression. Make it a good one, full of warmth and fun.

Greetings

A good responsibility for children is to post them at the gate or door to greet all new arrivals.

At that time new arrivals receive a program of all events, times and places for meals and other activities, what their responsibilities are, and any instructions or directions they might need.

No one should miss anything by not knowing about it.

We don't assume that people will know what to do, or where everything is located, for this may be the first visit for some.

Name Tags

Our young greeters enjoy giving out the name tags. Identifying people is important. Children change as they grow up and recently-married spouses like Douglas, Lisa, John, and Joey feel lost among all their new relatives. One time we gave everyone a gray cap using an illustration of The Wayside corner posts, with the name and date of the reunion on the front where advertisers usually put their information. Then we embroidered each person's first name on the cap's bill.

We soon discovered that a single name isn't really enough. There are duplicate Ruths, Bills, Davids, Beths, Anns, and others. One time we used neck scarves color-coded to families. The scarf with "John" embroidered on it that John Russell poked into his shirt pocket was blue, identifying him as Ralph's son-in-law, not pink for Ellen's son-in-law John.

Another time we put a number beside the name which stated the order of entering the family, either by birth, marriage, or adoption.

We started with our parents, giving them both number one. That made the oldest child, Miriam, number three, the third to enter the family. Carolyn bragged that she was a perfect Number Ten!

As the family increased, even identification by name and family wasn't enough to keep the relationships straight.

New generations popped up. On the year of the summer Olympics, we designed round cardboard "medals" to hang around the neck with different colored ribbons to identify the family. On the medal, we drew flowers to identify the generation and under the full name, gave the family relationship.

Hanging on a green ribbon for Vernon's family and with three flowers to show the third generation, this is what Roy's medal looked like:

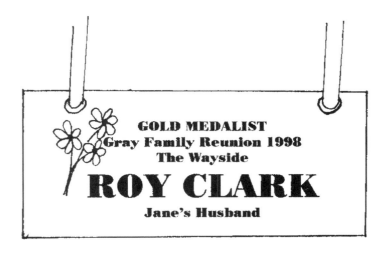

The medallions were successful. Everyone kept them on for the entire three days. Quite a record, we think.

Meals

Do not underestimate the importance of meals. Using caterers or restaurants, plan ahead for variety (remember vegetarians and special diets). Each person bringing a dish doesn't work for longer reunions, and no one should spend the whole time in the kitchen cooking. Buffets work well to get variety and save time with large groups, though be alert to those who may have trouble going through the line, like small children or older people. Let them go through first and sit in favored spots.

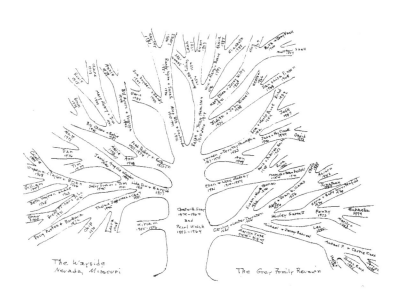

Most meals can be informal, but we've found that at least one all-together, sit-down meal is valuable. An emcee like Harold or Chet can conduct a general get-acquainted program where each family can introduce its members and bring the others up-to-date on their news. Sometimes we have all of Kathryn's family come up to stand behind her at the podium. At other times, Chet asks all of Gertrude's family to stand where they are and be introduced. Joking, anecdotes, and reminiscences flow over the room. Family-tree place mats (see diagram) at each setting will help everyone understand the relationships and become a souvenir to take home. When other activities resume, everyone feels more connected.

Activities

The most important components of the reunion are the planned activities. Some that involve a specific age group can be scheduled concurrently. Those that involve everyone will have no competition in that time slot.

Some examples of concurrent activities are: wading pools and other equipment for very small children, swimming in the pond, 10K runs, volleyball, croquet, looking through Bill's telescope, or a religious observance by Lester if on Sunday. Depending on the location, tours of the farm and local attractions, and antique shopping are popular. For more lengthy activities either before or after the reunion favorites are canoe trips and exploring ancestral homesteads.

It is important to provide for and welcome the very small children. We look forward to Gillian, Cicelie, Matthew, Michaella, Jerron, Gray and Caitlyn being old enough at the next reunion to join in the games.

The following activities are on-going. At one time or another, we have done each of these.

Plan some work that needs to be done, like painting one side of a building or wheelbarrowing sand to make a beach at the pond.

Make provision for displays of people's work. Harold labeled such a display "Ego Alley" when we set up tables in the drive-through area of the granary and asked people to bring evidence of something they've done, like published an article, painted a picture, or won awards.

Provide an opportunity for everyone to write an autograph in white paint on the blank back of the red barn.

All of the above are fun, but the most memorable activities are those we all do together. For example: family skits, talent shows, campfire singing, and tale-telling, Sally's most recent update on family genealogy research, square dancing, and playing modified versions of Jeopardy and Trivial Pursuit using questions and answers about the family.

One year when everyone was in the rented tent, shaded from the hot July sun, Ellen conducted a family quiz. First she passed out paper cups. Then she asked questions about who had experiences similar to the family's early days. For instance, since both parents taught school, she asked those who had ever taught school to raise their hands. There were quite a few to get an award for that. Penny, Kevin, and Michael passed around a tray of small candies, nuts, and raisins. Each one who raised a hand took a piece and put it in the cup.

Other questions were, "Who was born in Missouri?" "Who has children? Take one piece of candy for each child you have." And not to give an advantage to immediate family members, "Who was not born in Missouri?" "Who is here for the first time?" "Take a piece of candy for every brother and sister you have." You get the idea. Creative questions can stimulate interest and be fair to all.

Ellen planned questions so that at the end

everyone would have some goodies in his cup. The one with the most pieces won the prize, a handmade quilt with each family member's name embroidered in a color-coded block. The kids who passed the tray got to eat up the rest of the candies.

A test of a good reunion is that it will be over too soon. Fathers and mothers must get back to their jobs and responsibilities. The compensation is that everyone will look forward to the next one. After people hug goodbyes and wave as they drive down the lane, the planning committee can relax. That is they can if they remembered to plan for someone besides Michael and Carrie to stay and help clean up!

AFTERWORD
A Parting Thought

Did you notice how often we used the word fun? We even went through the manuscript and tried to substitute other words to avoid the repetition. Then we realized. Hey, that's what this is all about. It is about having fun with the family. If a game is not fun it is not a good game.

There are many different types of fun. The slap-happy hilarious fun that goes with silly games is one type. Quiet reflective enjoyment is another. And in between there are various intensities of amusement. But they are all fun.

Sharing these moments of fun within a family or any other group creates memories that last a lifetime. When the fun times can also enrich family lore, help us get better acquainted, and increase our mental or physical abilities, the fun multiplies.

We've had fun all our lives playing games. We had fun writing this book. We hope you will have fun using it.

So, let's all have fun!

BIBLIOGRAPHY

The following books are those in the Gray family library some dating from the early 1900s. In addition to traditional games handed down through the family and from neighborhood activities, these are some of the references we used to find new games, which then became part of our collection.

Bancroft, Jessie H. *Games for the Playground, Home, School and Gymnasium*. Macmillan Press. 1925.

Brown, Douglas. *150 Solitaire Games*. Dream House. 1993.

Esar, Evan. *Laugh While You Learn and Learn While You Laugh*. The Comic Encyclopedia, Doubleday. 1978.

Espy, Willard R. *The Game of Words*. Bramhall House. 1931.

Fluegelman, Andrew, Ed. *The New Games Book*. Doubleday/Dolphin 1976.

Hapgood, George. *Home Games*. The Penn Publishing Company. 1911.

Hollister. *Parlor Games*. The Penn Publishing

Company. circa 1905.

Meyer, Jerome S. *More Fun for the Family.* Greenberg Publisher. 1938.

Newell, William Wells. *Games and Songs of American Children.* Harper and Brothers. 1911.

Orlando, Louise. *The Multicultural Game Book.* Scholastic Professional Books. 1993.

Rice, Irvin. *Noncurrent Games, Games Played before Electronics.* pamphlet. 1998.

University of Missouri Extension Service. *Recreation Leaders' Handbook.* 1992.

Van Hagen, Winifred, Dexter, Genevieve; Williams, Jesse Feiring. *Physical Education in the Elementary School.* California State Department of Education. 1951.

Wells, Amos R. *Social Evenings.* United Society of Christian Endeavor 1907.

Wood, Clement and Goddard, Gloria. *The Complete Book of Games.* Garden City Publishing Co., Inc. 1940.

Index